100 GREATS

LANCASHIRE
COUNTY CRICKET CLUB

'O my Hornby and my Barlow long ago'

These famous lines come from the best known of all cricketing poems. Lancastrian poet Francis Thompson visited Old Trafford on many occasions, including the match against the Champion County Gloucestershire in 1878, whose side included the Grace brothers.

Hornby and Barlow were superb athletes and all-round sportsmen who opened the Lancashire innings for seventeen years with great success. The memorable partnership was nostalgically remembered by the mystic poet Francis Thompson some thirty years later when he was invited to watch his team at Lord's. He refused the offer for, without his famous heroes, it could never be the same, and the poem reflects his thoughts.

At Lord's

It is little I repair to the matches of the Southron folk,
Though my own red roses there may blow;
It is little I repair to the matches of the Southron folk,
Though the red roses crest the caps, I know.
For the field is full of shades as I near the shadowy coast,
And a ghostly batsman plays to the bowling of a ghost,
And I look through my tears on a soundless, clapping host
As the run-stealers flicker to and fro,
To and fro:–
O my Hornby and my Barlow long ago!

It is Glo'ster coming North, the irresistible,
The Shire of the Graces, long ago!
It is Gloucestershire up North, the irresistible,
And new-risen Lancashire the foe!
A Shire so young that has scarce impressed its traces,
Ah, how shall it stand before all resistless Graces?
O, little red rose, their bats are as maces
To beat thee down, this summer long ago!

This day of seventy-eight they are come up North against thee,
This day of seventy-eight, long ago!
The champion of the centuries, he cometh up against thee,
With his brethren, every one a famous foe!
The long-whiskered Doctor, that laugheth rules to scorn,
While the bowler, pitched against him, bans the day that he was born:
And G.F. with his science makes the fairest length forlorn;
They are come from the West to work thee woe!

It is little I repair to the matches of the Southron folk,
Though my own red roses there may blow;
It is little I repair to the matches of the Southron folk,
Though the red roses crest the caps, I know.
For the field is full of shades as I near the shadowy coast,
And a ghostly batsman plays to the bowling of a ghost,
And I look through my tears on a soundless, clapping host
As the run-stealers flicker to and fro,
To and fro:–
O my Hornby and my Barlow long ago!

Francis Thompson

100 GREATS

LANCASHIRE
COUNTY CRICKET CLUB

COMPILED BY
KEITH HAYHURST

TEMPUS

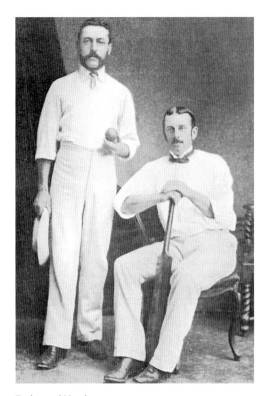

Barlow and Hornby.

First published 2004

Tempus Publishing Limited
The Mill, Brimscombe Port,
Stroud, Gloucestershire, GL5 2QG

www.tempus-publishing.com

British Library Cataloguing in Publication Data.
A catalogue record for this book is available from the British Library.

ISBN 0 7524 2405 X

Typesetting and origination by Tempus Publishing Limited
Printed in Great Britain by Midway Colour Print, Wiltshire

Introduction

The Manchester and Liverpool cricket clubs were formed in the early 1800s and regular matches were arranged between the clubs from 1826. Several matches were organised under the title 'Gentlemen of Lancashire' and in 1864 the first match under the name of 'County of Lancashire' was arranged. The 100 players featured in this book took part in matches from that date. The Old Trafford ground was chosen as the county headquarters with a pavilion for the amateurs at the north end of the ground and another built for the professionals on the opposite side near the railway.

In the early years most of the outstanding players were amateurs. They were businessmen, lawyers and other wealthy professional gentlemen, including the Rowley brothers, Appleby, the Steel brothers, Vernon Royle, Sam Swire and A.N. Hornby. An occasional bowler was employed as a professional cricketer.

An early Lancashire team consisting of mainly amateur players was as strong as any in the country but business commitments frequently tested the amateurs' priorities and in the first few years these gifted players chose not to play in ordinary county games, weakening the side. They made themselves available for important fixtures, including England matches.

In the 1880s a talented, balanced Lancashire team was winning the Championship under their influential captain A.N. Hornby. His enthusiasm, great authority and perceptive leadership brought the team together under one roof in the main pavilion, although there were still separate dressing rooms for amateurs and professionals. The aristocratic Archie MacLaren carried on the success in that golden age of cricket.

All the England Test matches for the first twenty-two years were held only in London and Manchester, the first at Old Trafford being in 1884. It was the second England venue after The Oval. Lord's became the third.

The most successful period of Lancashire's dominance was between the wars, when they won the Championship five times in a row and were unbeaten for the whole season on two occasions.

Main pavilion used by amateurs

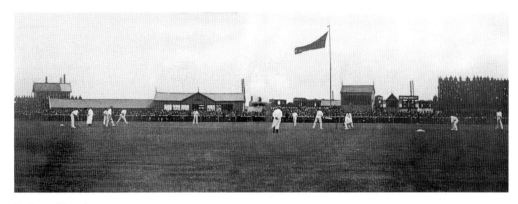

Professionals' pavilion.

In the last thirty-five years Lancashire has been the most successful one-day cricket side, winning seventeen major trophies.

Choosing the best 100 players is always a personal view. One cannot compare different eras fairly, as playing conditions have changed so greatly. Each era has produced great players and statistics will not tell the whole truth. To select one's best Lancashire XI from players representing the club over 140 years, as I have attempted below, is arguably an even more difficult task. The best side has to be balanced and I have allowed only one overseas professional. Players have been judged in their peak years.

Archie MacLaren (captain) Brilliant RHB. A tactical expert regarded by contemporaries as England's best captain.

Cyril Washbrook Forceful, prolific RHB. Holds opening stand record with Hutton for England in all Tests. Excellent cover-point fielder.

J.T. Tyldesley Aggressive, quick-footed RHB with excellent defence. For ten years the best professional batsman in England.

Ernest Tyldesley Elegant and prolific scorer RHB, brother of J.T. Tyldesley. Scored 100 first-class centuries averaging 45 runs in career.

Eddie Paynter Powerful, brave LHB. Averaged 59 in Test matches, an average of 84 against Australia.

Allan Steel Gifted all-rounder, brilliant right-arm medium-pace and slow spin bowler, attacking RHB and excellent fielder. A successful England captain.

Johnnie Briggs A very successful slow left-arm bowler, taking over 2,200 wickets, and an attacking RHB scoring over 14,000 runs. An excellent fielder and Lancashire's most prolific all-rounder.

Wasim Akram Overseas choice because of balance to team. Best left-arm fast opening bowler of his era. A good LHB to strengthen team.

Warren Hegg Most catches in Lancashire's history and still rising. Solid RHB and exceptional team member.

S.F. Barnes Regarded by most cricket historians as the best right-arm medium-pace bowler ever. He could turn the ball both ways with speed and bounce.

Brian Statham Best right-arm fast bowler to play for Lancashire, claiming more wickets than anyone. He took 2,260 wickets at an average of 16.

Under serious consideration were the following: Clive Lloyd, Neil Fairbrother, George Duckworth, Atherton and Crawley, Cec Parkin, Dick Tyldesley, Ted McDonald, Walter Brearley and maybe James Anderson and Andrew Flintoff in the future.

Lancashire Captains

Edmund Rowley
1864-79

A.N. Hornby
1880-93, 1897-98

Sydney Crossfield
(joint captain) 1892-93

Archie MacLaren
1894-96, 1899-1907

Gerry Bardwell
(joint captain) 1899

A.H. Hornby
1908-14

Myles Kenyon
1919-22

Jack Sharp
1923-25

Leonard Green
1926-28

Peter Eckersley
1929-35

Lionel Lister
1936-39

Jack Fallows
1946

Ken Cranston
1947-48

Nigel Howard
1949-53

Cyril Washbrook
1954-59

Bob Barber
1960-61

Joe Blackledge
1962

Ken Grieves
1963-64

Brian Statham
1965-67

Jack Bond
1968-72

David Lloyd
1973-77

Frank Hayes
1978-80

Clive Lloyd
1981-83, 1986

John Abrahams
1984-85

David Hughes
1987-91

Neil Fairbrother
1992-93

Mike Watkinson
1994-97

Wasim Akram
1998

John Crawley
1999-2001

Warren Hegg
2002-present

100 Club Greats

John Abrahams
Paul Allott
Arthur Appleby
Mike Atherton
Ian Austin
George Baker
Bob Barber
Richard Barlow
S.F. Barnes
Bob Berry
Jack Bond
Frank Booth
Walter Brearley
Johnnie Briggs
Glen Chapple
Geoff Clayton
Lol Cook
Ken Cranston
J.C. Crawley
Willis Cuttell
Harry Dean
Phillip Defreitas
George Duckworth
Jack Dyson
Peter Eckersley
Geoff Edrich
Farokh Engineer
Neil Fairbrother
Bill Farrimond
Andrew Flintoff
Graeme Fowler
Harold Garnett
David Green
Leonard Green

Tommy Greenhough
Ken Grieves
Charlie Hallows
Jim Hallows
Frank Hayes
Jimmy Heap
Warren Hegg
Ken Higgs
Malcolm Hilton
Len Hopwood
A.H. Hornby
A.N. Hornby
Nigel Howard
Bill Huddleston
David Hughes
Jack Iddon
Jack Ikin
Peter Lee
Peter Lever
Lionel Lister
Clive Lloyd
David Lloyd
Graham Lloyd
Ted McDonald
Bill McIntyre
Archie MacLaren
Harry Makepeace
Peter Marner
Peter Martin
Gehan Mendis
Arthur Mold
Muttiah Muralitharan
Buddy Oldfield
Cec Parkin

Eddie Paynter
Eddie Phillipson
Harry Pilling
Richard Pilling
Winston Place
Dick Pollard
Geoff Pullar
Bill Roberts
E.B. Rowley
Vernon Royle
Jack Sharp
Ken Shuttleworth
Frank Sibbles
Jack Simmons
Reggie Spooner
Brian Statham
A.G. Steel
Frank Sugg
Roy Tattersall
Ernest Tyldesley
J.T. Tyldesley
Dick Tyldesley
Albert Ward
Cyril Washbrook
Wasim Akram
Mike Watkinson
Alex Watson
Frank Watson
Alan Wharton
Len Wilkinson
Alan Wilson
Barry Wood

The twenty who appear here in italics occupy two pages instead of the usual one.

John Abrahams
LHB & OB, 1973-88

Born: Salt River, Cape Town, 21.07.1952

Matches: 251

Batting:

Runs	HS	Av	100s
9,980	201*	29.7	14

Bowling:

Wkts	Av	BB
56	50.1	3-27

Catches: 162

Born in Cape Town, John's father Cec Abrahams brought his family across to England, where he was engaged for many successful years as a professional in the leagues. John was therefore born in a cricketing environment. 'Abey' was a most enthusiastic, athletic cricketer, small in stature but one of the quickest and most useful right-arm off-break bowlers. He had much to offer first-class cricket. He possessed a determined nature, an inner strength and a positive, pleasant and bright outlook on the game. Making his maiden century against Yorkshire at Old Trafford at the age of twenty-four, it seemed he had cemented his place in the side. A partnership of 168 with the talented and aggressive Frank Hayes was made, Abey hitting 19 fours. It was another five years before he scored a regular 1,000 runs a season, averaging almost 40 in his best year of 1983, and adding 16 valuable wickets as an accurate off-spinner.

A series of big-name internationals had captained the county, and after three years of Clive Lloyd, the management believed Abey was a worthy leader. There were other Test players well established in the side who felt they should be given the role. It was not a simple task to captain a team of strongly opinionated, confident individuals.

Winning the Benson & Hedges Trophy at Lord's in his first year as captain showed his leadership qualities. Peter May presented Abey with the man of the match award for his overall control and the quality of his leadership. Members watching his two years as captain saw him succeed in building good team spirit with his seemingly easy, outgoing personality. Never seeking individual publicity, there was a dignity and integrity throughout his performance and a steely thread running through his character. Neil Fairbrother was witness to this when, reaching 94 on his debut innings, John declared. An arrangement had been made with Warwickshire to declare at a score and, keeping his word, he risked criticism on himself for robbing Neil of his maiden century.

In his first year as captain, he made his highest first-class score, an unbeaten 201 at Nuneaton. Replaced as captain after two years by David Hughes, Abey produced some fine batting performances in late season to almost clinch the Championship.

There are many different pieces that fit into the jigsaw picture of John Abrahams. He had a total of over 10,000 first-class runs, 56 wickets for his county and over 160 memorable catches as a brilliant fielder, but more importantly he was a great ambassador for the game. His natural ability to relate well with others helped to make him a much respected coach with the newly formed England academy.

Paul Allott

RHB & RFM, 1978-91

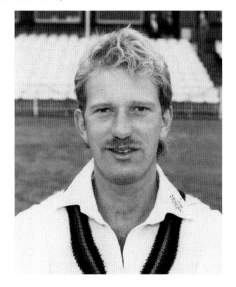

Born: Altrincham, 14.09.1956

Matches: 205

Batting
Runs	HS	Av
2,877	88	16.9

Bowling
Wkts	Av	BB
549	24.4	8-48

Catches 121

Tests 13

If the hand of a medium-fast bowler projects a ball from around eight feet from the ground, the batsman expects bounce and an awkward delivery. At 6ft 3ins, Paul Allott had accuracy in line and length as well as movement off the seam.

Paul's father, an enthusiastic club cricketer, saw his son progress from Altrincham Grammar School into the England Schools side and tour the West Indies with the Under-19 England team which included David Gower and Mike Gatting. He represented Cheshire in the minor counties at nineteen years and entered Durham University where Graeme Fowler and Gehan Mendis were studying. Some cricket was wedged into a busy schedule, including the UAU Championship.

Making his Lancashire debut at Bristol at twenty-one years, he took 5 Gloucestershire wickets in the match. Over a relatively short period of time he opened the bowling with either Colin Croft, Patrick Patterson or Michael Holding, a formidable trio from whom he picked up the principles of success. His career's best analysis of 8 for 48 at Northampton was made in 1981 when he was Lancashire's most successful wicket-taker with 85 first-class wickets. Noticeable performances nudged the selectors and he made his England debut the same year at Old Trafford, taking 4 wickets in the match and scoring an unbeaten half century to help retain the Ashes.

In 13 Tests for England his most successful analysis was 6 for 61 against the West Indies at Headingley in 1984. He played the same number of one-day internationals for his country.

Known as 'Walt' in the dressing rooms, he was relied upon by Lancashire for his trademark consistency, bowling a perfect off-stump line day in, day out. He loved the excitement of one-day cricket, especially Lord's finals. A reliable early wicket-taker and mean performer, he averaged 15 runs per wicket in the Gillette Cup and NatWest limited-overs games.

He was part of the first ever 'double' winning side of 1990 as well as the winner of three further Benson & Hedges and NatWest finals, a Refuse Cup winner and a John Player-sponsored National League title-holder

In county cricket, his most successful bowling performances were away from the Old Trafford batting track, including a 7-wicket haul for 72 against Somerset at Bath, 7 for 42 against Kent at Maidstone and 6 for 59 against Essex at Southend. Including a spell in Wellington, New Zealand, he took 620 first-class wickets averaging under 25.

After a healthy benefit in 1990, Paul carried on entertaining the public through his Sky TV broadcasting. On occasions he could be controversial, speaking his mind with a sharp tongue.

He was elected to the Lancashire Committee, where he served for six years, giving service back to the game that gave him so much pleasure.

Arthur Appleby

LHB & LFM, 1866-87

Born: Enfield, Lancashire, 22.07.1843
(d. 24.10.1902)

Matches: 58

Batting

Runs	HS	Av
1,052	99	13.3

Bowling

Wkts	Av	BB
245	12	9-25

Catches 44

The round-arm bowler projected the ball at the batsman from a horizontal straight arm at right angles to the body and not above shoulder height. This action proved to be too difficult for many cricketers, who bowled inaccurately with uncontrollable wides. Arthur Appleby had a strong physique and soon mastered the round-arm technique. He developed a graceful, easy action with an added advantage of being a left-arm bowler and relatively fast. His line and length were controlled and he could bowl for long spells without losing direction.

Training to be a manager in his father's corn mills, he played as an amateur for the 'Gentlemen of Lancashire' versus the Players of Lancashire. His performance was so impressive that he was invited to play in the Lancashire First XI versus Surrey at Liverpool on August 23, 1866. Taking 6 wickets for 30 runs in the first innings, he quickly established himself as a leading bowler. The following year he was opening the bowling with W.G. Grace for the Gentlemen *v.* Players at Lord's and achieved another 6-wicket haul in the first innings.

Business commitments as a mill-owner restricted his playing but, when he joined the team, Appleby made a difference. In 1871 at Sheffield he took 8 wickets and scored 99 runs, not realising he was close to a century. Captain

A.N. Hornby was waiting on the pavilion steps to present him with a new bat.

Appleby could not resist a short tour to America and Canada with the English amateurs in 1872, but turned down invitations to join Lord Harris' tour to Australia in 1878 and a later tour with W.G. Grace because of business commitments. An interesting letter in his scrap book from the American tour starts, 'My dear old Applepie,' and informs him that to the world amateur cricketers had to pay their own expenses but, confidentially, all costs were paid by the organisers and it would be more expensive staying in England.

Arthur Appleby was the leading amateur bowler in England for many years and on occasions topped the bowling and batting averages for Lancashire. He restricted his appearances to play in many more attractive games at Lord's. He remained loyal to his village club, Enfield, where he was twenty-five years as President, even playing for them a year before his death in 1902. As a member of the Lancashire and MCC Committees, a magistrate and an alderman, his popularity was evident on the day he was buried, with firms and schools in the Enfield area closed for the day.

Mike Atherton
RHB & LB, 1987-2001

Born: Manchester, 23.03.1968

Matches: 151

Batting:

Runs	HS	Av	100s
9,904	268*	44.4	29

Bowling:

Wkts	Av	BB
61	38.6	6-78

Catches: 126

Tests: 115

Scoring a match-winning 40 with style at the age of nine years playing for Manchester schools, it was reported that Mike Atherton showed unusual attacking and defensive qualities for his age. In his first appearance for Manchester Grammar School's Under-13 team he opened the batting and took 3 wickets bowling accurate leg spin. He occupied that opening position as batsman for five years, scoring 3,500 runs and taking 170 wickets. His leg-break bowling had remarkable control for his age, turning the ball sharply. Representing a powerful MCC youth side at sixteen years, he took 6 for 27.

Athers' early batting was technically correct and he showed a maturity with some delightful drives, particularly on the off side, moving quickly into line and severely punishing bad balls. His main asset was his lengthy concentration. As a captain, he was a shrewd tactician representing Lancashire Schools from eleven years old and England Schools from fifteen years. At that age, he won the Jack Hobbs Memorial Award as outstanding cricketer at Under-15 level. Mike led the Lancashire federation side for the Under-19 Championship when he broke the record aggregate of runs, scoring over 1,000 for the season. He first captained England Under-19 at sixteen years and made his Lancashire Second XI debut at the

same young age, scoring a half century against Yorkshire. At Youth level he showed commitment, dedication and an alert keenness, always arriving first for net practice and internalising good advice from coaches.

Making his first-class debut from Cambridge University with an unbeaten 73, his first century came a month later against Derbyshire at Fenners. His debut for Lancashire came against Warwickshire during the same season when his impact was immediate, sharing in a century stand of 364 at the Oval, only 7 runs short of the record partnership for any wicket. That season of 1990 was a special year. After captaining Cambridge in his last two years he was available to play for his county full-time, averaging 75 runs. Voted the Young Cricketer of the Year, he was one of Wisden's five cricketers. He took part in the first of two 'double' cup-winning sides, which was repeated in 1996. His first Test century came against New Zealand at Trent Bridge in that same special year of 1990. Another century followed against India at Old Trafford later in the season. He was the youngest Lancastrian to score a Test century.

This was his first appearance as an opener at Test level, having made his Test debut against Australia the previous season. Going in first, he showed a maturity beyond his youthful appearance. His immaculate technique, patience, concentration and shot-selection cemented his future position. England needed his ideal temperament to create a solid start. He topped the England averages with 71.

His leg-break bowling was developing as a further asset and in that 1990 season he took 6 for 78 for his county against Nottinghamshire. He captured 42 wickets that season, averaging 26 per wicket.

An inflammatory back condition was beginning to restrict his movement, and both Lancashire and England were to miss his spinning artistry alongside his accomplishment as a batsman. He seldom turned his arm after 1990.

The connoisseur and purist watching the county game appreciated his batsmanship. Athers never favoured impetuous haste. Building an innings, he stroked the ball through the covers and executed that favourite cut reaching high on his toes and cracking the ball past gully to the boundary. He liked to play the ball at the last moment, patiently waiting for the delivery that drifted towards his legs and then clipping it to the square-leg boundary. Although he appeared in 54 one-day internationals, making 12 centuries, his style suited the longer game where he had more space to show his craftsmanship.

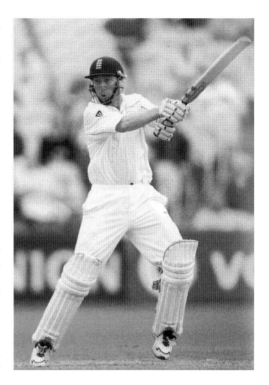

Athers captained England from 1993 for 54 Tests, more times than any other cricketer. He assured his place in the history of our great game with his epic performance in Johannesburg in 1995/96. For almost eleven hours he defied a gifted and confident South African Test team who tried everything to dismiss him. His exceptional powers of concentration and devotion to the cause kept the constant barrage of attack at bay, a Rorke's Drift-like achievement. The sporting public in their millions followed his progress at intervals from their work place. It inspired and lifted morale and earned him national affection. In his time he faced a parade of exceptional international bowlers who prized his wicket above all others. After 115 Tests and 7,728 runs for England, the whole Australian team stood to clap Athers as he left the field for the last time.

He never purposely sought to impress his public. Athers was once fined for having dirt in his pocket to dry his sweaty hands instead of bending to wipe them on the dusty turf. It seemed an energy-saving act, but the authorities did not agree. He enjoyed the dressing room banter and camaraderie, holding strong views about the game, and being sometimes critical of its inefficiency and future vision. He was also a quiet family man, well-read with a wide variety of interests which included fly fishing, appreciation of painting, music and good wine.

Lancastrians will remember him as a dependable, patient opening batsman. His highest score for the county was an unbeaten 268 against Glamorgan. He equalled Clive Lloyd's 6 centuries in Roses matches. Averaging 44 for Lancashire, Athers scored 21,929 runs in all first-class cricket. We will remember those elegant shots around the wicket which made him one of the finest English batsman of his generation.

Ian Austin
LHB & RM, 1987-2000

Born: Haslingden, 30.05.1966

Matches: 124

Batting:

Runs	HS	Av	100s
3,778	115*	27.9	2

Bowling:

Wkts	Av	BB
262	30.3	6-43

Catches: 35

Born in the Lancashire Pennine town of Haslingden, 800ft above sea level, 'Oscar' captained the town's high school team and joined the local club. It was not long before he created a new amateur batting record, an unbeaten 148 for the Lancashire League side. Playing for the Lancashire County Second XI, he helped win their Championship in his first regular season. In 1991, Oscar broke the Sunday League record with a total of 58 wickets averaging only 17. Playing in Australia for three winters broadened his experience.

Oscar loves the camaraderie of the dressing room. He is a dependable, enthusiastic and honest cricketer with a quiet, uncomplicated approach to the game. Broad-chested and with huge muscle-bound arms and calves, Oscar can crack a ball over the boundary with ease. Also nicknamed 'Bully' in the dressing room, his strength is an asset in all his sporting activities. With a controlled competitive attitude, he is an excellent team man, never seeking individual attention but keen for the team to win trophies.

Lancashire, with Oscar, did just that, visiting the final of a major cup competition eight times in ten years. His first trophy was won in 1989 when the first Refuge Cup was won at Edgbaston. Oscar was a regular in the side and the following year he was an essential part of the double-winning side, the first county to win both cup competitions in a season. They

repeated that feat in 1996. Austin's accurate, swinging deliveries were highly valued. Oscar bowled right-arm medium pace so tightly, his statistics were astonishing – 4 for 21 from his allotted spell in the final of the Benson & Hedges Cup against Northamptonshire won him the Man of the Match and 3 for 14 from 10 overs in the NatWest final against Derbyshire in 1998 won him the same award, making him the first player to achieve the gold award in both competition finals. The next day Lancashire won the Sunday League and finished runners-up in the Championship. He was picked to play limited-overs cricket for England in 1998 and took part in the World Cup of 1999.

There were many highlights in his Championship cricket too. He scored the fastest century of the season in a Roses game at Scarborough in 1991, the following year scoring another against Derbyshire in a stand of 178 with his pal Warren Hegg. He holds a Lancashire record for the 7th wicket with Graeme Lloyd when they put on 248 against Yorkshire at Headingley.

A talented all-round sportsman, he spent two years at Burnley FC in his youth and many hours at Baxenden Golf Club. Possessing the natural build of a rugby forward, some of the fitness experts and dieticians suggested he lost weight from his muscley, stocky frame. Oscar's answer was 'look at the records' and he never let the side down. His immense popularity among the members was manifested in his super benefit total of well over £150,000.

George Baker
RHB & RM 1887-1899

Born: Malton, 18.04.1862 (d. 06.02.1938)

Matches: 228

Batting:

Runs	HS	Av	100s
7,170	186	22.3	4

Bowling:

Wkts	Av	BB
138	25.1	6-18

Catches: 142

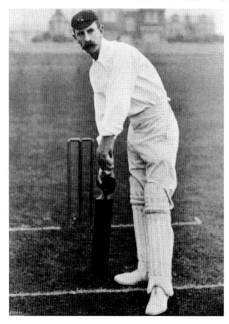

The speed limit on roads for motor vehicles was 14mph as Britain celebrated Queen Victoria's Diamond Jubilee in 1897. That year, Lancashire won the County Championship. A major influence in this achievement was the excellent batting of George Baker. A tall and slim figure, he was a right-hand batsman who played a handful of games for Yorkshire without success before moving to Bury as their league professional in 1885. From there his career took off and he was called into the Lancashire side two years later at twenty-five years of age.

In that jubilee year he scored over 1,200 runs for the county on open pitches that were often difficult for batsmen. A series of high scores, particularly away from home, included 140 to beat Hampshire at Southampton and 186 against Sussex at Hove to win by an innings. He was a forceful player with a wide selection of strokes all round the wicket. He was chosen to play for the Players who beat the Gentlemen twice with a strong batting side including Abel, Tom Hayward, W.G. Quaife, George Hirst, William Gunn and Arthur Shrewsbury. His score at The Oval against the Gentlemen was a top score of 87 in the innings, dismissed by W.G. Grace. He played with and against the best of the day.

Baker was a good, keen fielder and a more than useful medium-pace seam bowler. He was a partnership breaker, a second-change bowler. Under favourable bowling conditions he took 6 for 18 in 22 overs in 1896 against Gloucestershire at Bristol to win by an innings in spite of W.G. Grace remaining on an unbeaten century. The same year he took 5 for 35 from 13 overs at Trent Bridge to win by an innings after his batting contribution of 84, the top score.

Enjoying his cricket wherever he played, he was popular with colleagues because of his pleasant disposition. He kept links with the town of Bury, opening a sports outfitters there. After retiring from playing with Lancashire at the turn of the century, he took an appointment at Harrow School as coach for twelve years. He moved on to Leighton Buzzard as groundsman and greenkeeper for Anthony de Rothschild.

George Baker was a keen all-round sportsman, a useful rugby footballer and a competent athlete. He appreciated his good fortune in being able to earn a living from his passion. In later years he suffered poor health but, loyal to all his clubs, he kept in contact by visiting them in turn until his death at seventy-five years of age.

He will be remembered for his all-round contribution to Lancashire's success and his selection for the Players team over a five-year period. Scoring over 7,500 first-class runs in a stylish manner and taking 145 wickets with 153 catches confirms his all-round ability.

Bob Barber

LHB & LB, 1954-62

Born: Withington, Manchester, 26.09.1935

Matches: 155

Batting:

Runs	HS	Av	100s
6,760	175	28.2	7

Bowling:

Wkts	Av	BB
152	31.3	7-35

Catches: 70

Tests: 28

Achieving the feat of 1,000 runs and 100 wickets in a season as a schoolboy is indeed rare at such a young age. As a pupil at Ruthin School in 1953, many coaches witnessed outstanding potential fulfilled at an early age. The following year, Bob Barber played for the county of his birth, making his debut at No.6 against Glamorgan at Old Trafford as an eighteen-year-old amateur. Expectations were high for this intelligent all-rounder.

The following season he continued the progression by winning a blue at Cambridge for cricket and, proving his all-round sporting ability, added a blue for throwing the javelin. He opened the batting successfully, left-handed, fearless of fast bowling and with a full repertoire of strokes all round the wicket. He was a talented leg-break bowler and an excellent fielder, particularly in the led trap.

In 1960 Bob was proud to accept the captaincy at a time when the team was in transition. The Committee believed in strong leadership and took some of the responsibilities of selection which would be less acceptable today. Lancashire led the Championship table in August after completing the double over Yorkshire but the last six matches were disastrous and the club finished second. Barber's own contribution was good, scoring well over 1,000 runs and taking 47 wickets including 7 for 35 at Chesterfield against Derbyshire.

The Committee decided to dismiss three first-team players at the end of the first season. Differences were aired in the press and it was thought by some that with his courteous and sensitive nature, Barber may have taken the role too early. The following season saw the county slip down the table to thirteenth, although the captain's own performances remained consistently good. The Committee believed the captaincy was handicapping his development as an international player and in 1962 appointed Joe Blackledge, an experienced league player, as captain. Less success for the county followed and Barber decided to make a fresh start with Warwickshire in 1963 and quickly developed into the spectacular player shown in his early years.

Bob Barber was never lower than the top four in the Lancashire batting averages when playing regularly. He averaged almost 30 with the bat and took 152 wickets for his county. He was chosen for England against the South Africans in 1960 going on to play 28 Tests. He was one of the five Wisden cricketers in 1967.

His developing business interests in the north took precedence and after a takeover he retired to Switzerland a wealthy man. He visits Manchester occasionally and keeps in touch with his colleagues at Old Trafford.

Richard Barlow
RHB & LM, 1871-91

Born: Bolton, 28.05.1851 (d. 31.07.1919)

Matches: 249

Batting:

Runs	HS	Av	100s
7,765	117	20.3	2

Bowling:

Wkts	Av	BB
736	13.6	9-39

Catches: 197

Tests: 17

In the latter part of the nineteenth century, Dick Barlow was one of Lancashire and England's prominent all-rounders. Naturally left-handed, his father convinced him that all left-handed batsmen appeared awkward so he changed to right-handed but continued to bowl left arm medium-paced . The Lancashire side in the 1880s was fortunate to be gifted with some aggressive, swashbuckling amateur batsmen. Barlow, the professional, was given the job of opening with his captain, the ebullient Hornby. Dick was a more serious, careful batsman with a sound defence and complete concentration and was instructed to keep his wicket, an anchor role, while the amateurs were allowed to show flair. W.G. Grace wrote that Barlow had 'the patience of Job' and found him difficult to dislodge. The Lancashire opener was a fitness fanatic, an athlete who could run as fast as any player in his side. His place was to secure a sound base, allowing the gifted amateurs around him to take the limelight. Barlow responded by carrying his bat through the innings thirty times. In the end his county average was only two less than the seemingly more prolific Hornby. The two are made famous through the game's most lyrical poem 'At Lord's' by the mystic poet Francis Thompson, whose nostalgic line 'O my Hornby and my Barlow long ago' placed them into immortality.

For a period Barlow opened the batting and bowling for England. He deserved his place for his bowling skills alone, supported by his immaculate fielding at point. Barlow's left-arm spinners displayed a complete mastery of line and length and his deliveries varied from slow turners to fast off-breaks and a ball that shot through with the arm beating the batsman with speed. He dismissed the formidable W.G. Grace more times than any bowler except Shaw of Nottinghamshire.

The popular Barlow was welcomed by large crowds at Manchester Central station on his return from the Test matches in Australia in 1883. His contribution to all matches was vital, particularly his 7 for 40 in the second innings at Sydney which clinched the Ashes.

In the autumn of 1884 the Australian touring side played the North of England team at Trent Bridge in a three-day match. The Australians had a formidable team led by

W.L. Murdoch. The famous fast bowlers Spofforth, Palmer and Boyle all played, as did prolific batsmen Bannerman, Giffin, the massively-built Bonner and wicketkeeper Blackham. The North of England side, full of star players, included Barlow of Lancashire. Spofforth, the demon bowler who had terrorised the English, inspected the wicket and announced he would bowl the Englishmen out for 60! Barlow's performance was magnificent. He scored a faultless century in 4 hours 25 minutes. The last man out, he was immediately given the ball to open the bowling. He took 10 wickets in the match, beating the Australians by 170 runs. Murdoch, the Australian captain, was so impressed with Barlow's performance (111 for once out, 10 wickets for 48 runs in the match) that he took off his cap and presented it to Barlow saying, 'I take my cap off to you'. The headlines in the press, 'I take my hat off to you' were where the phrase originated from. Barlow's cap is in the Lancashire Club museum – a priceless item of memorabilia.

Barlow was the first major collector of cricket memorabilia. His home in Blackpool housed an extensive collection of bats, photographs, trophies, medals and personal memorabilia presented to him for his many accomplishments throughout his distinguished career. He played for Bolton, his birthplace, when he was twelve years old. He took a wicket with his first ball in first-class cricket against Yorkshire and went on to take three hat-tricks for Lancashire and another for Players v. Gentlemen which included the top English batsmen, W.G. Grace, John Shuter and W.W. Read. Barlow made three tours to Australia with the England side, playing in 17 Test matches including the first ever at Old Trafford, the second ground to hold a Test match after The Oval. A supportive crowd of 26,000 people came through the gate to give him a massive benefit match against Nottinghamshire in 1886 to prove his popularity. Lancashire presented him with a stained-glass window depicting Barlow at the wicket, Pilling behind the wicket and Hornby by his side. The three played in the first Test at Old Trafford. This most famous stained-glass cricket window is on display in the Old Trafford pavilion.

Barlow retired from first-class cricket too early after twenty years with Lancashire. He took up first-class umpiring and stood in W.G. Grace's last Test in 1899. It was his breadth, variety and success in many sports that made him unique. He won prizes in athletics as a sprinter and hurdler and was good enough to turn professional. He played football, keeping goal for his county, and as an FA referee he officiated at Preston's cup-tie in 1887 when North End defeated Hyde 26-0, it is still a record score in the FA Cup.

Dick Barlow continued to play as a professional cricketer for league clubs: Royton in Lancashire for seven years and Blackpool where he bought a large home to house his collection. He was a dealer in sporting goods and claimed to be the first to introduce rubber-faced wicketkeeping gloves and single-strap leg guards. He designed wicket gloves, an airtight valve and a laceless football. He would say that no cricketer could have enjoyed his career more than him. This most interesting and talented Lancashire cricketer designed his own gravestone which stands in Leyton cemetery near Blackpool. It shows a representation of a bat falling to the ground in front of a wicket broken by a ball. Underneath is inscribed 'Bowled at Last'.

S.F. Barnes

RHB & RM, 1899-1903

Born: Smethwick, 19.04.1873 (d. 26.12.1967)

Matches: 46

Batting:

Runs	HS	Av
452	35	11.8

Bowling:

Wkts	Av	BB
225	19.8	8-37

Catches: 20

Tests: 27

In the opinion of his contemporaries, S.F. Barnes was the best bowler in the world. Australian and English batsmen voiced that opinion unanimously. Most still consider him to have been the best ever. A tall, lean but elegant figure with stern face, he set his field with flicks of his long first finger. A shortish run to the wicket with long springing strides, arm brushing the ear, he bowled a vicious fast leg-break from the front of the hand, like his off-break, the only first-class bowler to do so. Contemporary batmen said they could not read his action. He could swerve the ball in the air, vary the pace, spin it both ways and with his advantageous height, achieve lift and accuracy. Never was a delivery wasted, every ball had to be played.

Sydney Barnes had an imposing presence, his face firm, all expressive of serious determination. He was a perfectionist, an independent, opinionated cricketer with an awkward temperament, reacting sharply when any fielder showed slackness in gathering a ball from his bowling. There was no touching the forelock to those in authority. He spoke his mind clearly and they had to earn his respect. He was not an easy man to captain, remaining mysteriously aloof, believing his leader had fewer skills than he.

S.F. signed for Rishton in the Lancashire League after taking three wickets for Warwickshire. The league club paid him £3 10s a week as professional and groundsman, with an extra bonus for good performances. In five years with the club he took over 400 wickets averaging 9 runs each. Moving to Burnley he achieved 100 victims each season and was invited to play for Lancashire. He entered first-class cricket at a time when one ball sufficed for the whole innings; there was no change of ball after 100 overs. The wise judgement of the Lancashire captain Archie MacLaren noticed his extraordinary talent and most controversially invited S.F. to play for England in the forthcoming tour of Australia. Criticised widely for picking an unknown and untried bowler, MacLaren trusted his judgement. Sometimes greatness needs opportunity, and his captain had provided this.

S.F. had never seen a Test match before he played in his first at Sydney, Australia. He was given the new ball and his second delivery turned to create a false stroke from the great Victor Trumper who was at his brilliant best. Barnes bowled and caught the great master, one of the best batsmen in the world, for his first Test wicket. He finished 5-65 in that first innings. In the Second Test he achieved 6-42 and 7-121, was overbowled and suffered a knee injury.

Born in Staffordshire, the only first-class county that can claim him as theirs is Lancashire, whom he represented for four

seasons. There was a clash of personalities with the strong-willed MacLaren, but his leadership nurtured the great talent and Barnes improved his tally of wickets each season, finishing with 131 wickets in his final season with the club, averaging 17.8.

Barnes soon came to prefer the rewards and comparative inertness of the weekend league matches to the daily toil of county cricket. Thousands came to watch the unsmiling destroyer, who was paid handsomely for outstanding performances. Working one day a week for the same wages and fewer clashes with authority suited him well. His knee injury soon cleared up and there is no doubt that he profited from playing comparatively little cricket which enabled him to keep fresh. Loyalty wasn't his greatest asset, for he would play for any club who offered him the greatest financial reward. He signed contracts with over a dozen league clubs as well as playing for Warwickshire, Lancashire, Staffordshire, England and Wales.

Although he took a record number of league wickets at an astonishingly low average, he should be judged by his performance against the best first-class cricketers of his day. S.F. took most of his Test wickets on the Australian pitches when they were perfect batting wickets. One example of his quality was in the Test at Melbourne in 1911. Australia won the toss and batted on a magnificent batting pitch. Barnes' first ball bowled Bardsley. Hill went next, clean-bowled for 4. Then Kelleway was bowled LBW by Barnes for 2 and the great Warwick Armstrong was caught at the wicket. Four of Australia's best batsmen were out for 11 and Barnes had all four for one run. After an hour, Barnes' analysis was 9 overs, 6 maidens, 3 runs and 4 wickets in conditions perfectly suited for batting. Considering the quality of opposition and conditions it is generally regarded as the greatest piece of bowling in the whole history of cricket, especially as he had been feeling unwell before the game and was unable to bowl after taking another wicket.

In South Africa two years later he was unplayable with 49 wickets in only 4 Tests, still a world record. He refused to play in the fifth match because the South Africans had not carried out their promise of a special reward if he took part in the tour. His haul of Test wickets was 189 at just 16 runs each.

Barnes remained a deadly bowler until the end. He played for Staffordshire at fifty-six years of age and took 76 wickets at only 8 runs each. In his favourable domain of league cricket he took an amazing total of over 4,000 wickets averaging only 6. In his last full season on the leagues he opened the bowling for Stone and began with 6 for 32. He was then sixty-seven years of age. In his mellowed years he agreed he had been an 'awkward cuss' but without question, the master of them all, unique, like a perfect gem.

Bob Berry
LHB & SLA, 1948-54

Born: West Gorton, 29.01.1926

Matches: 93

Batting:

Runs	HS	Av
427	27*	8.3

Bowling:

Wkts	Av	BB
259	22.7	10-102

Catches: 53

Tests: 2

Only three players have taken 10 wickets in an innings for Lancashire. The last occasion was at Blackpool against Worcestershire in 1953 when Bob Berry dismissed all 10 in the second innings for 102. His match figures were 14 wickets for 125. He had achieved almost the same match figures against Somerset at Old Trafford in the previous home match, 13 wickets for 124. That summer he took 98 first-class wickets averaging 18, his most successful season.

Born in West Gorton, Manchester, he was Lancashire to the core. Playing club cricket for Denton St Lawrence and Longsight before joining the county in 1948, he made his debut the same year. The club was oversubscribed with spinners, with Bill Roberts, the Hilton brothers and Roy Tattersall as well as Ikin and Grieves able to bowl leg-breaks. Test calls, injuries and spinning pitches all came into the formula and Bob Berry's left-arm spin showed enough guile to attract a contract.

It was his skilful variation in flight that deceived the batsman. It was not a vicious spin of the ball, rather a roll of the fingers and accuracy in length and variety of speed that helped Bob to take over 700 first-class wickets.

He earned himself a Test trial in 1950, taking 5 wickets against an England side. Bob did not lose his accuracy even when Hutton used every means possible in his long innings to try and destroy Bob's line and length. He was selected to play against the West Indies in the First Test at Old Trafford. The visitors brought a strong, talented side that included the three

Ws. They reached 50 without loss before Bob was put on to bowl in his international debut. With the bowling unchanged to the end of the innings, he finished the second innings with 4 for 53, an excellent debut for this intelligent bowler and the only win by England in the series. He was picked for the Second Test at Lord's, for which the famous calypso was written, when the opposition spinners Ramadhin and Valentine dominated. The following winter he toured Australia with the England side without playing in a Test match.

Competition for places in the Lancashire XI forced him to moved to Worcestershire and then to Derbyshire, becoming the first player to be capped by three counties. After retirement in 1963, Bob became a publican in Burton-on-Trent, then moved to hotels in Derby, Mansfield and finally Farnsfield where he became President of the local cricket club. He was honoured with the same position in the Lancashire Players' Association later in his life.

Bob Berry and Malcolm Hilton, both slow left-arm spinners for the club, remained good friends and when Bob lost his wife and Malcolm died, Bob married Vera Hilton to enjoy a successful second innings together at Farnsfield. Visiting Old Trafford regularly, he remains the same chirpy, enthusiastic, humorous character.

Jack Bond

RHB & Occas. LB, 1955-72

Born: Kearsley, 06.05.1932

Matches: 344

Batting:

Runs	HS	Av	100s
11,867	157	26.6	14

Catches: 217

Genuine affection surrounded Jack Bond as a leader. His popularity stemmed from the way he encouraged and nurtured players. As well as having a good cricket brain, he was a caring, understanding man of principles. His naturally coercive manner inspired a passive team into an efficient, successful unit. He was given the captaincy in 1968 as the limited-overs competitions were growing in popularity. His quick-witted humour strengthened team spirit. Of course he needed players with talent around him; astute captaincy was not enough on its own. The two together created the spark.

Born in the small Lancashire town of Kearsley, John David Bond played league cricket for Radcliffe. He joined Lancashire County Cricket Club in 1955 and soon proved to be a successful captain of the Second XI. Jack Bond's perceptive mind (Bolton School educated) and naturally warm nature planted the seeds, fed the growth and more than anyone enjoyed the blossoming of unexpressed talent. When given the First XI captaincy, the team climbed from eleventh to sixth in the Championship. Bond led by example, topping averages and setting new standards in fielding. Farokh Engineer and Clive Lloyd arrived and Lancashire won the John Player Sunday League in its first year of inception and repeated the success the following year, when Bond was

selected as one of Wisden's five cricketers. From 1970 to 1976 the nucleus of that team won 26 Gillette Cup matches out of 29, these being the longer 60-over games so popular among spectators. Thousands were locked outside the ground for the Gillette Cup semi-final against Gloucestershire in 1971 and so much interest was aroused that the match's progress was broadcast live on BBC TV prime-time news. Bond led Lancashire to the final and victory, repeating the success the following year, the first club to gain the hat-trick of wins.

Smaller than average in height, Jack was a naturally aggressive batsman who could hit the ball over a close field, drive well and use the speed of the balls, glancing and cutting behind the stumps. He was an excellent fielder, quick and fearless. In 1962, he scored over 2,000 first-class runs, including a century in each of the Roses games. A broken wrist from the West Indian fast bowler Wes Hall the following year affected his batting in future seasons.

On retirement, Jack became joint coach and after a couple of years with Nottinghamshire he returned to manage the first XI for seven years. Finally, he became a first-class umpire until retirement.

Being a brass band enthusiast, a former table-tennis champion of the Isle of Man where he coached youth cricket and a Vice-President of the Lancashire CCC keeps this generous and caring regular church-goer very busy.

Frank Booth

Born: Manchester, 12.02.1907 (d. 21.01.1980)

Matches: 140

Batting:

Runs	HS	Av
1,330	54	10

Bowling:

Wkts	Av	BB
457	24.4	7-59

Catches: 56

A tall, well-built, handsome chap, Booth had a long run and lumbering action. A right-armed bowler, he was medium-fast and the quickest on the Lancashire staff after McDonald retired in 1931. His success was due to the ball coming off the pitch sharply with bounce and, when conditions were right for him, he made it difficult for the batsman to survive. Of Pollard-like attributes, he was an indefatigable bowler who delighted in long spells. He was a great trier who was content to keep plugging away. Never seeming to tire, his long spells brought him rewards but also injuries.

Frank Booth was born in Cheetham Hill, Manchester in 1907. He made his debut at twenty years old, at first appearing only occasionally in the strong and settled First XI. Booth found turning out for the Second XI less rewarding than league cricket and he chose to play for East Lancashire in 1931. McDonald retired from Lancashire after that season and Booth returned to his county team finding himself in demand for a first-team place. He responded with 50 Championship wickets, bowling over 600 overs in the season. Not always given the opportunity to open the bowling, he showed his potential against Leicestershire by taking 4 wickets for 3 runs in 6 overs as second change bowler. Although a tail-end batsman, he could be aggressive on occasions, scoring a quick 50 against Kent at Old Trafford in 1933 and hitting a six and 4 fours which enabled his team to beat Kent.

The following season Lancashire won the Championship, Booth being instrumental in achieving that position. The team were undefeated all season and proud that, on occasions, it had fielded a side of players who were all born in Lancashire. Frank Booth took 100 wickets, achieving 5 wickets in an innings against Middlesex, Surrey, Somerset and Essex. He opened with Dick Pollard mostly, although Phillipson was emerging as an opener and there were successful all-rounders in Hopwood, Iddon and Parkinson.

Success remained with him the following season, and against Essex at Old Trafford he took 11 wickets in the match in 32 overs to win by an innings. Opening with Pollard against Gloucestershire, he took another 11 wickets at Gloucester, capturing 7 for 59 in the first innings. He dismissed the great Wally Hammond in both innings.

Frank Booth made his mark in Lancashire's history, particularly in achieving 100 wickets to help his county top the table. Loving the outdoor life, he retired to the South Coast, where he died in 1980.

Walter Brearley
RHB & RF, 1902-11

Born: 11.03.1876 (d. 13.01.1937)

Matches: 106

Batting:

Runs	HS	Av
749	38	6.1

Bowling:

Wkts	Av	BB
690	18.7	9-47

Catches: 44

Tests: 4

Neville Cardus described Brearley as a forceful wind blowing through cricket, a gale of humanity raising a merry dust in the process. In his short career, Walter Brearley made his unique mark in the history of Lancashire cricket not only as the best amateur fast bowler in England at that time but also as a notable character with a volatile temperament and inexhaustible vitality. He was born in Bolton and educated in Derbyshire at Tideswell Grammar School where the sportsmaster inculcated the love of cricket. Still in his youth, he returned to play in the Farnsworth Parish Church team, moving later to Bolton, Bury and then the Manchester Cricket Club. Sport was an enjoyable hobby and it took Walter some time to be an effective bowler. When he put bulk on his tallish frame he was invited to play at Lancashire as an amateur. He had entered the business world and with two of his attributes, hard work and determination, he was to make a successful career outside sport. Introduced to first-class cricket at twenty-six years against Sussex at Hove in 1902, he watched the great S.F. Barnes open the bowling and at first change Walter took a couple of wickets for 71 runs, a little expensive in good bowling conditions.

The following season was much more enjoyable. Taking note of S.F. Barnes' immaculate line and bounce, Walter took 69 wickets for his county in his second season. Barnes and he took all 20 wickets at Old Trafford, 10 each for less than 90 runs to beat Surrey by 7 wickets. The bigger the game the greater the challenge. Experiencing his first Roses game at Old Trafford, he opened the bowling, capturing 6 Yorkshire wickets for 81 runs. In his third season Lancashire won the Championship unbeaten. He was revelling in the team's success and produced some excellent performances.

At his peak, Brearley was a well-built right-arm fast bowler who generated great pace from a short run of 7 or 8 yards. He had great stamina, willing to bowl for long periods and finishing just as fast and dangerous at the end of play as he was in his opening spell. At 15 stones in weight, his short run was smooth and athletic, with no leap at the wicket and then a full windmill-like arm action. With powerful shoulders and a full follow-through, his body movement provided a perfect length and lift. He could swing the ball and on occasions cut it, the ball moving into the right-hand batsman from the seam. Varying his position of delivery from the crease, he troubled the best of batsmen and he experimented with line, swing and turn.

There was no dawdling when walking on to the field, just a brisk movement to the middle to start the day's business. He was impatient to start bowling out the enemy. With a fine constitution, he had an indestructible confidence, believing every ball would bring him rewards. MacLaren, his captain, put him in the genuinely 'great' class. When communicating that a change of bowling was appropriate, Brearley would nod at his captain and suggest he changed ends!

His batting seldom troubled the scorers. Always last in to bat, he would hurry to the wicket, sometimes vaulting the boundary fence. Often he would not bother to wear the protection of pads or gloves. The big man's intention was to slog the first ball out of the ground. On one occasion he reached 38 against Northamptonshire at Old Trafford, but his career average was just over 5. A very popular figure at Old Trafford, the crowds waited for his entrance. They looked upon him as a wonderful entertainer, cheering at his unusual antics and admiring his great bowling feats.

Although a genuine, likeable person, he could be quick to take offence even when none was intended. He had many disputes with the Committee, especially if he was not selected. Hornby as President and MacLaren as captain were equally unbending. Brearley resigned from the club on numerous occasions; returning after a winter had given him cooling-off time.

Walter was selected to play for England in 4 Test matches. At Old Trafford in 1905 he took 4 wickets against Australia. In all he took 17 Test wickets at 21 each. Dismissing the great Victor Trumper three times in Test matches that year and three more times in other games for less than 30 runs in total, Walter called the great man his rabbit! When not selected for a Test against Australia, he stationed himself below the MCC Committee at Lord's, voicing his opinion quite audibly about the injustice of leaving him out. The commotion caused the police to be called to move him on. In the 1909 season, Archie MacLaren approached him to play for England against the Australian tourists, but Walter, feeling the indignity of being left out of the original side, refused the invitation.

One of his best years was 1905, when some extraordinary bowling feats were achieved. At Old Trafford he took 17 wickets in the match for just 137 runs against Somerset. It was the first recorded occasion that a Lancashire bowler had achieved that total in one match. It included 4 wickets in 4 balls. The same season he took 7 for 115 in the first innings against a strong Australian side. At Old Trafford a crowd of 25,000 watched Brearley take 5 for 31 in the first innings of the Roses game, asking Yorkshire to follow on. At Sheffield he continued devastating the Yorkshire batting with 13 wickets in the match. In total that year he captured 181 wickets at 19 each. Three years later he took 163 wickets averaging 16 each. In all first-class matches his 844 wickets averaged 19 in what turned out to be seven full seasons with injuries and disputes. He was chosen as one of Wisden's five cricketers in 1908. MacLaren was right in his assessment of this great amateur bowler's talent. He could bring to life a slow, dead pitch and bowl a side out on a good batting pitch with his superb, natural skill, untiring energy and enthusiasm. Concentrating on his business commitments, he played occasionally for Cheshire after leaving the first-class game. His final first-class match was for an England XI against the Australians in 1921.

Brearley married the daughter of a hotelier at Bowness in the English Lake District. His business took him to London, where he coached the young schoolboys at Lord's every April until his death.

Brearley died aged sixty years and was buried at Bowness. There is no doubt that his devastating performances and unforgettable personality lit up cricket in Edwardian England.

Johnnie Briggs
RHB & SLA, 1879-1900

Born: Sutton-in-Ashfield, 03.10.1862
(d. 11.01.1902)

Matches: 391

Batting:

Runs	HS	Av	100s
10,707	186	19	9

Bowling:

Wkts	Av	BB
1,696	15.6	10-55

Catches: 185

Tests: 33

Born with abundant enthusiasm and energy, Johnnie Briggs developed the love of cricket from his father, James, a league professional at many clubs across the north of England. As a young boy Johnnie spent his summers at Hornsea Cricket Club where his father was professional for three years. At eleven years old the youngster had the experience of bowling in the nets to the champion cricketer W.G. Grace when the United South of England played a Hornsea XI. Grace was surprised at the accuracy of such a young bowler. Johnnie became the youngest ever professional for the same club at thirteen years of age. The following year he moved to Widnes with his family and shortly afterwards Johnnie was seen by Lancashire professional Dirk Barlow playing in a friendly match in Liverpool. He was invited to play for Lancashire at the early age of sixteen years.

Johnnie was an outstanding fielder and showed great potential as an all-rounder. His natural fast and accurate return of the ball saw him develop into a brilliant cover-point fielder. His youthful exuberance never left him throughout his life and he added to his exceptional fielding a brave, daring, free-hitting batting style as a right-hander. He then created the complete cricketer by developing an artful variation in his left-arm spin bowling. At only 5ft 5ins in height, his brief run-up of two joyful skips and a jump followed by an easy styled delivery produced a disguised variation of ball that broke both ways with changeable speed. He included a fast delivery that surprised the best players of his day, although his most destructive ball was a sharp leg-break.

An all-round sportsman, he played full-back for Widnes rugby union team until he broke an arm. He was a keen hockey player and very competent at billiards. His first love though was cricket, and by 1885 he was a regular in the Lancashire First XI. That year he married Alice Burgess at Farnworth Old Church, Widnes. Two days later he made his highest score of 186 for Lancashire against Surrey at Aigburth. Coming in at No.4, he hit splendidly but kept losing partners until last man Pilling joined him and they put on 173 for the last wicket. A.N. Hornby, Lancashire's captain, said he wished Briggs could always be on his honeymoon. Briggie said he was married to cricket as well as his patient wife Alice.

In 1888 Wisden featured six outstanding bowlers in the world of cricket. Top of the list was Briggs, who took 187 wickets that year with the best average of all, just 9 runs per wicket. He was regarded as one of the most able and destructive bowlers. That season included some phenomenal performances: 5 for 15 against the Australians at Old Trafford, 6 for 24 against Derbyshire, 13 for 73 against Middlesex and 13 for 40 against the Australians at Scarborough.

The following year W.G. Grace admitted that he preferred to stay at the non striker's end when Briggs took 7 for 22 at Bristol. Grace said he was quite unplayable, especially on a slow wicket. Briggie never wanted to be taken off. He bowled 630 deliveries in a match against Sussex, which is still a record for the county.

On August Bank Holiday in the early 1890s over 20,000 spectators swarmed into Old Trafford to witness the prodigious Roses match. Lancashire batted first, Briggs contributing a magnificent 115 which included 15 boundaries in two and a half hours. He followed his most entertaining innings by taking 13 wickets in the match to give his county an innings victory. The following year against Surrey at The Oval he scored 112, and then took 11 wickets for 115 runs on a fairly good batting pitch to give his county victory. This meritorious match double (a century and 10 wickets) was achieved for a third time. The same year a huge crowd at Old Trafford saw one of the most exciting finishes in the history of Roses matches. Yorkshire needed only 20 runs to win with 7 wickets to spare. Johnnie dismissed them and Lancashire won by 5 runs.

It was not only his brilliant performances that endeared him to the mill-working crowds that flocked to Old Trafford when he played: it was his comical, youthful exuberance and infectious enthusiasm which caught the popular mood. There was an immediate affinity with his audience. His antics were more the result of high spirits and intense interest in the game than any desire to show off. He always showed a passion and commitment which sometimes manifested itself in comical actions

which draw laughter from the crowd. No one got more fun out of the game or worked so hard for victory. He abhorred unsportsmanlike behaviour and was the most popular and loved of all cricketers. Johnnie was a special player.

At the age of twenty-two years, he headed the Lancashire bowling averages and the following season was called up to play for England at Lord's. Australia looked comfortable at the wicket and were scoring easily until Briggs bowled his first spell as an international cricketer. He performed magnificently, finishing with match figures of 11 wickets for 74 runs helping England to win by an innings. The bowler Briggs was becoming a household name at home and abroad. In South Africa he took 15 Test wickets in a day for just 28 runs, the only bowler to achieve that feat. Taking a hat-trick at Sydney and scoring a Test century at Melbourne, he became the only Englishman to do both against the Australians. Johnnie Briggs was the first bowler to take 100 Test wickets. He undertook six Test tours to Australia as well as the tour to South Africa.

In his career, he scored over 14,000 runs and took 2,221 wickets at an average of under 16. Statistically, he is Lancashire's most successful all-rounder by a long way.

During the Headingley Test match against Australia in 1899, Johnnie suffered an epileptic fit and was taken to Cheadle Asylum where he rested for a few months. Recovering the next season, he returned to play for his county and delighted his multitude of fans by taking all 10 wickets for 55 in the first innings against Worcestershire at Old Trafford. During the winter his illness returned and he died in Cheadle shortly afterwards at the young age of thirty-nine years. At his funeral the crowds assembled in their thousands to pay respect for their hero. They held up business and transport for hours until he was laid to rest in Stretford Cemetery. He will remain forever one of Lancashire's favourite sons.

Glen Chapple

RHB & RMF, 1992-present

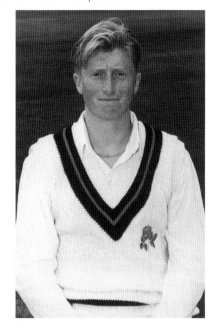

Born: Skipton, 23.01.1974

Matches: 153

Batting:

Runs	HS	Av	100s
3,798	155	23.5	4

Bowling:

Wkts	Av	BB
450	29.6	6-30

Catches: 49

Born into a cricketing family, Glen toured with the England Under-18 side before making his debut for Lancashire at Hove when eighteen years old. He opened the bowling with his long-term partner Peter Martin for the first time at Edgbaston, taking 5 wickets in the match. In the rain-affected game against Glamorgan the following summer at Old Trafford, the tail-end batsmen opened the second innings and were 'fed' by two batsmen seeking a declaration. Chapple, at nineteen years and never having scored a first-class 50, cracked the fastest century in first-class cricket from 27 balls in only 21 minutes. There were 34 hit in one over and the innings contained 31 fours and 10 sixes. 'Chappy' averaged 47 in the season.

The following summer he took 50 wickets, including 6 for 48 against Durham. Taking 5 wickets in an innings – more than any bowler for Lancashire that season – he was selected for the England 'A' Tour in India and again for England 'A' to tour Australia in 1996/97. As a right-arm medium-fast bowler, he can swing the ball away from the bat in English conditions. There are times when he achieves devastating spells and is rewarded with record-breaking figures.

After taking part in the successful Benson & Hedges Cup-winning team of 1995, the following summer he won the gold award in the NatWest Trophy final at Lord's against Essex. Putting the ball on the right spot, he recorded an all-time best performance of 6 for 18. No other bowler used the conditions as well.

Chappy played an important part in Lancashire's successful season of 1998, winning the National League title and the NatWest Trophy where he took 5-57 in the quarter finals. The National League title was won again the following year.

In 2000, consistency was evident with performances like 6-42 at the Riverside against Durham. The following summer he was Lancashire's highest wicket taker, with 53 wickets at an average of 22. In the match at Old Trafford he took 6 for 46 and scored 155 runs to equal the No.8 batting record. It was a superb innings where he looked as skilled as any batsman in the side. Moving up to No.6 in the batting order gave him the opportunity to show his all-round ability. He plays with a straight bat and has a variety of powerful shots, particularly the straight drive.

He consistently achieves the 500-run mark and 50 wickets a season. In 2002 he recorded his career best first-class bowling performance against Somerset at Blackpool with 6 for 30, and at Hove he took 10 wickets in the match against Sussex. Chappy has shown his worth and value to the Lancashire side with over 3,000 first-class runs and moving up to 500 first-class wickets.

Geoff Clayton

RHB & WK, 1959-64

Born: Mossley, 03.02.1938

Matches: 183

Batting:

Runs	HS	Av
4,382	84	19.2

Catches: 390

Stumpings: 32

An efficient wicketkeeper who missed little, Geoff was born in Mossley, 150 yards from Micklehurst Cricket Club where he played as a twelve-year-old. Selected for Lancashire Schoolboys, he quickly progressed to England Schoolboys at fifteen years while playing for Ashton, then Werneth Cricket Clubs. Leaving school, he joined Lancashire's youth team, playing for the Second XI at eighteen years. National service called and after playing for the Army he made his first-class debut for combined services at Worcester. His Lancashire debut came against Yorkshire in a friendly at Middlesbrough when he was twenty-one. In the same year he showed his quality as a keeper in a match against Gloucestershire when he caught 8 and stumped 1 batsman, a record for Lancashire until Hegg surpassed it thirty years later. After he was capped, he dismissed 92 batsmen in a season; only George Duckworth had bettered that total, over thirty years before.

A small man at 5ft 5ins but sturdily built, he was nicknamed 'Chimp' because of his posture. He could be contentious and never courted popularity, especially with amateurs. Chimp was never comfortable with authoritarians. Technically one of the best wicketkeepers in the country, he stood up to the medium-fast pace of Colin Hilton or Freddie Moore. A natural, perceptive keeper, he positioned himself expertly in the right place, with the experienced slips often taking a guide from him. He was efficient, unobtrusive and a determined fighter, never giving up the struggle to win.

Chimp was his own man. He loved the camaraderie of the dressing room, never happier than when involved with a card game. He never sought female company, he would choose his own mates and enjoy a cigarette and a few pints after the game. In the winter, he was a coalman, working for a coal merchant friend. His hobby was greyhound racing and he became a professional trainer and was well known around the north Manchester circuit for his hounds. He drove them around in his old ungainly van, which fitted his own caricature as a wheeler and dealer. But Chimp was a kind man, generous in nature and sympathetic to young players. As a keeper he read the game well and could give valued advice but had little time for those he felt knew little of the game.

A useful right-hand batsman, Chimp scored an unbeaten 74 against Middlesex at Old Trafford and 84 at Hove. Believing he was a disruptive influence, he was dismissed from Lancashire after the 1964 season and joined Somerset for three years. In his first season there he scored a century against Middlesex and was capped by his second county. His full first-class record included over 6,000 runs and 668 dismissals as a keeper, the majority for his home county.

Returning to his home in Mossley, he is involved in looking after severely handicapped people as a volunteer. Knee problems have limited his work and he visits Old Trafford when he is able.

Lawrence 'Lol' Cook

RHB & RMF, 1907-23

Born: Preston, 28.08.1885 (d. 02.12.1933)

Matches: 203

Batting:

Runs	HS	Av
2,051	54*	12.2

Bowling:

Wkts	Av	BB
821	21.3	8-39

Catches: 136

A rounded, jovial figure, Lol Cook made his mark in Lancashire's bowling history as a right-arm medium-pace bowler who could spin the ball into the right-handed batsman with striking accuracy. His strength of arm and perfect line and length surprised many opposing batsmen. His first ball in county cricket clean-bowled the experienced Wilfred Rhodes. Before batsmen learnt of his unexpected cut-back, he finished with 5 for 46 in his first spell. More superb performances followed in his first year, 5 for 61 against Worcestershire, 8 in the match against Derbyshire and 11 in the match at Canterbury.

Lol's father was groundsman at Preston and the youngster played league cricket for Lytham, being paid junior professional wages. He was keen to make a living out of sport. In the winter he played soccer and eventually played a few games for Blackpool and Preston North End. In cricket his great love was bowling and when conditions were a little damp he could be devastating, as the first innings 8 for 39 at Northampton proved.

The war came just as all his experience and skills were combining and he was robbed of vital years which may have made him great.

His most prolific performances came after the war. In 1919 he was third in the averages and the following year captured 150 wickets at under 15 runs each. Batsmen were surprised at the speed of the pitch and misread the slower ball which spun and lifted. That year he took 10 wickets in Harry Dean's benefit game against Kent, 10 wickets against Gloucestershire, the same against Sussex and 12 against Nottinghamshire. At Chesterfield his miserly first innings spell brought 7 wickets at under 22 each. Lol Cook bowled almost 1,300 overs during the season but loved the work as unemployment soared in the depression years after the war. He appreciated his good fortune in being paid for doing what he loved best and it stimulated him to take another massive haul of wickets each season.

In his late thirties he moved to the lucrative Lancashire leagues to be professional at Rawtenstall where he is still remembered with affection. Lol's brother Billy played cricket for Lancashire and football for Preston and Oldham. Lawrence himself was given a generous benefit game in 1923 against Middlesex when 30,000 people paid at the gate to support him, the winning hit made at ten minutes to seven. Lol managed to prolong the game as long as possible. It brought him £1,657 to set him up in a second career, but he died ten years after retiring from Lancashire cricket.

Ken Cranston
RHB & RMF, 1947-48

Born: Aigburth, Liverpool, 20.10.1917

Matches: 50

Batting:

Runs	HS	Av	100s
1,928	55*	40.1	2

Bowling:

Wkts	Av	BB
142	23	7-43

Catches: 32

Tests: 8

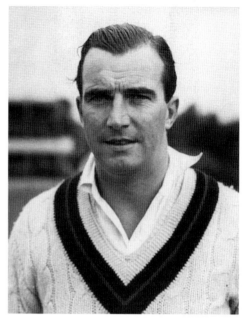

In an extraordinary career of only 2 full seasons, Ken Cranston scored over 3,000 first-class runs and took nearly 200 wickets, including 4 wickets in an over for England at Headingley against South Africa. He captained Lancashire for both years; played 8 Test matches against 3 countries, including Australia; and captained England in the First Test against the West Indies at Barbados.

A dentist whose hobby was playing cricket at the weekend for Neston in the Wirral, Ken Cranston had no ambition to play cricket full-time. He was more interested in making a career from his profession. Cricket every day would have bored him, he told me on numerous occasions. His outstanding ability as a cricketer was proved in early games against public schools and universities. On occasions he was invited to play for Lancashire Seconds, scoring the occasional century.

Continuing his profession in the Navy as a surgeon Lieutenant, many invitations came to play cricket during the war. In 1942 he scored a brilliant unbeaten century at Aigburth against the Army and the same year he played for the British Empire XI, scoring a century at Uxbridge and hitting 13 fours and a six in an excellent display of driving and cutting.

In his thirtieth year, Ken Cranston was invited to captain Lancashire and he made his first-class debut against Oxford University at The Parks in 1947. Proving his class, he shared in a partnership of over 150 with Winston Place. In his first home game against Kent at Old Trafford, he was Lancashire's top scorer and took 5 for 32 in 22 overs to win the match easily.

His all-round ability and pleasant manner earned him popularity with his fellow professionals. He would seek their advice and was a good listener. Cranston looked the part, a distinguished, cravatted, tall, handsome cricketer who led by example. In his second season he achieved his best bowling figures: 7 for 43 (10 in the match) against Surrey at The Oval. He scored over 1,000 runs each season and opened the bowling attack on several occasions. He was a seam bowler just above medium pace. Never out of the top five in the batting or bowling averages for Lancashire, he led them to third and fifth place in the table in consecutive seasons.

Returning to dentistry and captaining Neston on a Saturday, he did make an appearance in September the following year playing for the MCC against Yorkshire and scored an unbeaten 156. It seemed a wasted talent, but would the same freshness and motivation have remained through long seasons? President of the Lancashire Club in 1993/94, he is still a regular visitor to Old Trafford showing a keen interest in the game he graced so sparingly.

John Crawley

RHB & RM, 1990-2001

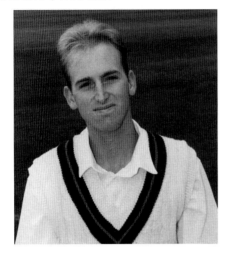

Born: Maldon, Essex, 21.09.1971

Matches: 138

Batting:

Runs	HS	Av	100s
10,533	281*	51.1	31

Bowling:

Wkts	Av	BB
1	187	1-90

Catches: 93

Tests: 29

Born in a cricketing environment, with his father and uncle good league cricketers and two brothers who played first-class, John was the most gifted of all. His elegant, wristy stroke-making style made him a most attractive right-handed batsman to watch. He is the only Lancashire player to average over 50 in his career for his county. A prolific run-maker from his youth, he averaged 156 in his final year at Manchester Grammar School. Captaining the England Under-19s, he became the first to score 1,000 runs in Under-19 Tests.

After making his debut for Lancashire at eighteen years against Zimbabwe at Old Trafford, he studied for a history degree at Cambridge. In his University debut he scored 83 against Lancashire, making his maiden century for them the following year against Oxford University. In 1992, J.C. produced a cultured innings scoring a glorious 172 opening the Lancashire innings at Lytham. The England selectors were nudged on many occasions, including his magnificent 286 for the England 'A' team on their tour of South Africa. Voted the Young Cricketer of the Year and topping the Lancashire averages in 1994, there was one innings among many that stood out. On a wearing pitch at Southport, he scored a brilliant 281 against Somerset. It was the second highest individual score for Lancashire since the war.

Called up for England against South Africa for the Lord's Test, he made a nervous start. His expected high scores did not materialise at Test level and he seemed to lack confidence against quality fast bowlers. Recalled to play against Sri Lanka in 1998, J.C. faced a prime bowling threat of Muralitharan and scored a majestic 156, driving purposefully off his legs, batting for five and a half hours. He could play spin bowling as well as any player. His leading foot was placed straight down the pitch, which meant he was stronger on the leg side.

His brilliant batting for Lancashire continued, frequently suppressing the county bowlers and in 1998 he scored 1,850 runs, heading the national averages and making 400 runs more than any other player, overseas included.

Made captain the following year, he helped Lancashire to win the National League and gain second place in the Championship. County cricket suited him best, where he thrived and entertained with well over 10,000 runs and the high average of 51. He never achieved the same in limited-overs competitions or Test cricket.

Success was a vital ingredient for J.C. He withdrew into his shell if his form faltered. The Committee felt that captaincy was affecting his batting and the role was offered to Warren Hegg. Crawley believed a move of counties would be beneficial and he joined Hampshire where his early form reappeared at county level.

He will be remembered for his aesthetically pleasing free style; a long innings by him was always memorable.

RHB & LB, 1896-1906

Born: Sheffield, 13.09.1864 (d. 09.12.1929)

Matches: 213

Batting:

Runs	HS	Av	100s
5,389	137	20.4	5

Bowling:

Wkts	Av	BB
760	19.5	8-105

Catches: 128

Tests: 2

The first Lancashire player to achieve the double (1,000 runs and 100 wickets in a season) was Willis Cuttell. His father had played a handful of games for Yorkshire but the son, unable to gain a place in the first-class game, came to the Lancashire leagues to earn a living. After a spell with Accrington, he settled in Nelson, helping them win the championship four times.

The right-armed Willis Cuttell was not just an accurate medium-paced bowler – his tremendous success would never have been achieved without other skills as a bowler. With a beautiful action he delivered a quick leg-break to turn the ball away from the watchful right-handed bat and then with the next ball produced a brisk off-break to keep him attentive. The captain, A.N. Hornby, said his best ball was one that went straight on with the arm. All three were delivered with an exceptionally accurate pitch and, more surprisingly, with no apparent change of action. There was variation of pace too, and often the quicker ball, lower in flight than most spinners of his day, surprised the experienced batsman.

His bowling performance for Nelson was impressive enough to attract Lancashire's attention. He was invited to join the county side at thirty-two years of age and, playing alongside the greatest of Lancashire's all-rounders, Johnnie Briggs, Lancashire won the Championship in 1897. Cuttell's all-round ability, achieving the double the following year, earned him a place with Lord Hawke's team in South Africa. Making his debut with J.T. Tyldesley, he played in both Tests, batting at No.5 and taking 6 wickets altogether for only 12 runs each.

Under Archie MacLaren's captaincy, Cuttell became a first-rate all-rounder with excellent fielding; some hand-hitting as a middle-order batsman added to his accuracy as a bowler. Among his many good performances for Lancashire, Cuttell took 8 for 105 against Gloucestershire at Old Trafford, dismissing W.G. Grace twice. He took 7 for 19 against Derbyshire and playing for the North against the South he took 8 wickets for 41 runs in the match, clean-bowling W.G. Grace in both innings. His highest score was 137 against Nottinghamshire at Old Trafford and before he had retired he scored nearly 6,000 runs and took almost 800 wickets.

Willis Cuttell returned to the warm, friendly people of Nelson. Moved by the affection and encouragement of this very special cricket community, he carried on playing as an amateur and working in the mills as a warp dresser. His modest benefit money from Lancashire and Nelson allowed him to purchase a corner tobacconist shop in the town where he lived for the rest of his life, among the people who gave him his early inspiration.

Harry Dean
LHB & LFM, 1906-21

Born: Burnley, 13.09.1884 (d. 12.03.1957)

Matches: 256

Batting:

Runs	HS	Av
2,448	49*	10.3

Bowling:

Wkts	Av	BB
1,267	18	9-31

Catches: 115

Tests: 3

Sixth in the list of all-time wicket-takers for Lancashire, Harry Dean from Burnley was many bowlers in one. His main attack was left-arm medium-fast, but his variations included slow spin and he used movement through the air effectively with more pace. He was broad-shouldered, over six feet tall and possessed a workaholic attitude. That was necessary, because he had phenomenal success until the war years cut his promising career short.

Dean took 100 wickets in every season from 1907 until the war came. He played little after 1920 when he achieved his last 100 wickets and was granted a benefit against Kent. On a two-day match he was rewarded with £2,217, a small fortune in those days, showing the great respect in which he was held.

When Dean was at his peak at twenty-seven years he was the top wicket-taker in the country with 183 wickets at 17 runs each. He bowled well over 1,200 overs in a gloriously hot summer. The wickets were one inch lower than today's height and although most victims were caught, a good number were clean-bowled. He opened the bowling with Walter Brearley, another workhorse, and sometimes Lol Cook or the spinner Huddleston. At twenty years of age he averaged a remarkable 12.5 for his 136 wickets. This was a poor sea-

son for weather, much wetter, and Dean used his spin variety, taking 15 wickets in the Old Trafford game against Kent.

In 1912, Dean made his Test debut in the Triangular Series against Australia and South Africa. Australia were dismissed for 65, Dean taking 4 for 19, and at Headingley he captured 5 for 56 against South Africa.

King George V visited Liverpool in 1913 and a match was held at Aigburth to celebrate the grand occasion. Dean achieved the rare analysis of 17 wickets in the match for 91 runs. No bowler from either side has recorded greater success in a Roses game. Walter Brearley and he are the only bowlers to have achieved this remarkable feat playing for Lancashire.

Other notable figures include a match at Old Trafford in August 1909 against Somerset, whom he demolished taking 9-31. Five batsmen were clean-bowled. He achieved 9 wickets in an innings six times. The following season he took 16 wickets in the match against Somerset at Bath. He took over 1,300 wickets in all first-class matches. A tail-end batsman, he averaged just over 10 in his career.

Harry Dean had too much to offer the game when he retired from Lancashire in 1921 and he went on to play for Cheshire and finally coach at Rossall School. He died in the lovely Lancashire village of Garstang aged seventy-one years.

Phillip Defreitas
RHB & RFM, 1989-93

Born: Dominica, 18.02.1966

Matches: 76

Batting:

Runs	HS	Av	100s
2,314	102	24.6	2

Bowling:

Wkts	Av	BB
231	29.9	7-21

Catches: 25

Tests: 44

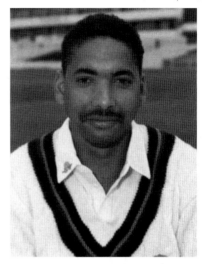

Born on the small West Indian island of Dominica, 'Daffy' arrived at his British school at the age of ten. After a spell on the Lord's ground staff he was offered a contract at Leicestershire and on his debut impressed with 5 for 39 against Lancashire. After four years with the Midlands club he moved to Lancashire and in his first season bowled out Middlesex at Lord's in 10 devastating overs, finishing with 7 for 21.

Bustling with natural aggression, this tall, athletic bowler at his best could move the ball both ways off the seam. He was first seen as a right-arm strike bowler, but lacked consistent control. Bowling within himself, he developed into a more accurate medium-fast, and his confidence grew with added success in all types of cricket. If conditions suited him he could be a match winner, but he needed some assistance from the pitch in Championship games before he would stretch himself. He was the only bowler who had taken over 1,000 wickets in first-class cricket by the 2001 season, some achievement in a reduced Championship programme.

His swing bowling suited the limited-overs game and he proved his worth for Lancashire in his second season in the NatWest final at Lord's. In a brilliant spell of 8 overs, 4 of them maidens, and with 5 wickets for 19 runs, he virtually won the game for Lancashire and was presented with the Man of the Match award. In one-day games for Lancashire he took 150 wickets and in his career was awarded 9 Man of the Match awards. Daffy also played over 100 one-day internationals for England, capturing 115 wickets.

Taking 7 wickets for 70 against Sri Lanka in their solitary Test at Lord's in 1991, Daffy took 30 Test wickets in the 6 Tests played that season, topping the England averages. He was rewarded by being chosen as one of five Wisden cricketers in 1991. Playing 44 Tests in total, he averaged 33 from his 140 wickets and scored almost 1,000 runs. Touring Australia three times, he played Tests against India, Pakistan, New Zealand, Sri Lanka and the West Indies.

If the mood suited, Daffy could score highly as a middle-order batsman with some explosive displays of hard hitting. In his second year for Lancashire he scored a quality century against Oxford University. The same season he made a valuable unbeaten 75 against Hampshire. It seems his batting talent was unfulfilled with too few high scores. In his last move back to Leicestershire he hit a brilliant century against Lancashire at Grace Road. Playing against his former colleagues provided the motivation.

Brilliant in the field with a flat, accurate throw, he could win any match on his own but showed his all-round skills too infrequently. He always lived life to the full, a colourful cavalier cricketer who will be remembered in Lancashire for his excellent one-day bowling performances.

George Duckworth

RHB & WK, 1923-38

Born: Warrington, 09.05.1901 (d. 05.01.1966)

Matches: 424

Batting:

Runs	HS	Av
4,174	75	14.6

Catches: 634

Stumpings: 288

Tests: 24

Travelling out to Australia for the infamous Bodyline series, Lancashire and England wicketkeeper George Duckworth was anxious to be alone and found a secluded spot on the top deck of the SS *Orontes* where he proceeded to read his book. Presently the ship's bore discovered him: 'Are you Mr Duckworth?' George sighed and nodded.

'From Lancashire?' He nodded again with an 'mmm...'

'Oh that's interesting. I've got an uncle in Lancashire.'

'That's nowt,' said George, 'I've got six.'

Duckworth was born, bred and died in Warrington, Lancashire. His father was a wicketkeeper for the town's cricket club for twenty years and George, being the eldest of ten children, learned to shout the loudest. He transferred both family skills to the keeper's role and was Lancashire's first choice for fifteen years. A by-product of his tremendous enthusiasm was the loudest appeal in first-class cricket. No one was allowed to ignore George, his presence was stimulating and the batsman knew he had a dangerous foe behind as well as the approaching bowler.

There was an overt zest about this stocky keeper; he clattered the stumps on appeal. Sharp eyes and quick hands earned him international respect. He kept to the best – regularly McDonald of Lancashire and Larwood of England as well as the spin of Cec Parkin and Dick Tyldesley. The Australian captain Montague Noble, who observed Duckworth, wrote of him: 'he bustles along between overs as eager to continue the strife as a boy is to ride his first bicycle and his youthfulness and enthusiasm appeal to the crowd.'

In fifteen seasons of first-class cricket, he claimed over 1,000 victims, including a rare feat of over 100 in one season. He should have added more to his 24 Tests because he was a better keeper than Les Ames, but not in the same league as a batsman so the latter was chosen as an all-rounder for England. Any sense of injustice was tempered by the positions of his good friend Bill Farrimond of Lancashire Seconds and England. It was an untimely period for both of them when Lancashire had two high-class keepers not wishing to leave their beloved county.

George played in five Championship sides, his best was the 1928 season when he made 107 dismissals. Only two keepers in the history of the game have taken more, Les Ames and Hugo Yarnold. Eight dismissals were taken in a match twice, the first time against Kent in his record breaking 1928 season and secondly against Warwickshire at Old Trafford in 1936.

Possessing a quick wit and good humour, he was always popular with colleagues. A determined, fidgeting little batsman, he could be difficult to dislodge. His partnership with Iddon in 1929 put on 198 against Leicestershire at Liverpool in just two and a half hours, George's contribution being 75, the second-highest score of the innings. In his career he scored almost 5,000 first-class runs. Highly respected by supporters, he was awarded a benefit match against Surrey in 1934 and received £1,257. His house cost him £300, so in the context of his day, it was a valuable reward.

Always an enthusiast, he was willing to try any activity and on his retirement from Lancashire he went into radio commentary, analysing competently both cricket and rugby league, his second passion. George was a director of the Warrington rugby league side and was a keen follower of all their winter matches. He tried hotel management and even farming, turning his hand to anything that was available.

George's vast knowledge of cricket, built up over years of watching closely behind the stumps, enabled him to be a shrewd judge of a player. He was invited to manage three Commonwealth touring sides to India, Pakistan and Ceylon from 1949 to 1954. Enjoying the experience, he followed those duties by becoming baggage-master and scorer at home and abroad where his popularity and wise judgement was sought by individuals of

the team. He was well known for creating a good team spirit.

Statistically he is Lancashire's most successful keeper with 921 victims and in total, 1,090 dismissals in all first-class cricket. His vitality and warm, generous nature always wished to serve the game in later years, although he died at the relatively young age of sixty-four. As a member of the Lancashire Committee, I'm sure his regular appeals were heard and came as passionately as those from behind the stumps.

Jack Dyson
RHB & OB, 1954-64

Born: Oldham, 08.07.1934 (d. 16.11.2000)

Matches: 150

Batting:

Runs	HS	Av	100s
4,433	118*	21.4	1

Bowling:

Wkts	Av	BB
161	27.6	7-83

Catches: 55

Oldham-born Jack Dyson was an all-round sportsman who achieved some success as a batsman and bowler for Lancashire. In the winter he played inside forward for Manchester City and was presented with a winner's medal in the 1956 FA Cup final at Wembley when Bert Trautmann played on with a broken neck. Dyson scored the second goal.

It was in 1956 that Jack created a cricket record with Alan Wharton in a match against Leicestershire at Old Trafford. Declaring after passing the Lancashire total, they won the match without losing a wicket in either innings, the only occasion in first-class cricket when this has happened

Werneth was Jack's club on leaving school and he was invited to join Lancashire, making his debut at nineteen years against Glamorgan at Swansea. In his third year with the club he was promoted to opening batsman and scored his maiden century against Scotland at Paisley. He made 1,000 runs that season and showed promise as a youngster who could play straight with a sound defence and accumulate runs rather than show flamboyance in style. His football career with City affected his cricket as

he broke a leg before the 1958 cricket season and was unable to play all summer.

At twenty-five years of age, Jack was improving his off-break bowling to add to his all-round sporting skills. At average height he learnt to spin the ball slowly from an accurate length using a little variety in direction. As an off-break bowler he achieved some successful performances, especially on a drying wicket. Taking over 50 wickets in the 1959 season, he continued his success the following year, achieving his best bowling analysis of 7 for 83 against Somerset at Taunton. In that match he also scored 100 runs for once out to demonstrate his all-round abilities.

There was a difference of opinion between him and Lancashire captain Bob Barber, which resulted in his dismissal until re-engaged in 1963. The new one-day competition sponsored by Gillette had started and Dyson was given another chance as an all-rounder. He proved his worth in the second game against Essex at Old Trafford when he top-scored with 60 runs and took 5 wickets for 47 from 13 overs. He surpassed the performance of his international bowling partners Statham, Higgs and Lever on that day, winning the gold award for Man of the Match.

Leaving to play for Staffordshire in 1964, he struggled to make a living when his sporting days were over. He was a regular at Old Trafford until he died at the early age of sixty-six.

Born: Newton-Le-Willows, 02.07.1904
(d. 13.08.1940)

Matches: 256

Batting:

Runs	HS	Av	100s
4,588	102*	18.5	1

Bowling:

Wkts	Av	BB
1	145	1-7

Catches: 113

Lancashire saw leadership potential in this young Cambridge graduate from his early days. He was eighteen years old when he made his debut for Lancashire at Fenners, although he was never selected for the Cambridge XI. In his second year with Lancashire, while still at Cambridge, he scored a century for the Second XI. Eckersley was proving his leadership qualities in judging the men in his team and drawing out their best qualities. He was twenty-three years old when he captained the side for one match at Blackpool. The match was won. It was a strong, well-balanced team that won the first of three Championships in consecutive years.

Gradually improving his batting performances, Peter Eckersley scored his maiden century at Bristol in 1927. The same season he was stumped on 99 at Bournemouth. He was a risk-taker, occasionally becoming restless and keen to move the score on. He drove hard and used his feet well against slower bowlers but he had a slight weakness in defence, often being bowled out rather than caught. Athletic in the field, he instilled enthusiasm and a positive attitude.

The following season was completely wiped out because of an operation for appendicitis. It gave him time to think of his future and he became a prospective Parliamentary candidate for his local Newton division. The Lancashire Committee persuaded him that the captaincy

of his county would open more doors, and he withdrew from his political interest to be captain of his club at the age of twenty-four years in 1929. He held the post for seven years as well as serving on the Lancashire Committee as an amateur captain, an unusual move as a player.

Peter was a popular leader, not having the distant presence of Major Green, his predecessor. In his second season as captain, the team won the Championship. They won it again in 1934 without a match-winning bowler; that year his captaincy was a major asset. Everyone performed under his direction. He was a lucky leader, too, winning the toss on 24 occasions.

In his final season (1935) he chartered two private planes to take the team from Swansea to Southampton. He retired with a record of over 5,600 first-class runs, averaging almost 20, and 21 catches. His last game was for an England XI but he was already a Conservative MP for the Exchange Division of Manchester, won at the 1935 election. When war broke out he joined the air division of the RNVR and was killed in a flying accident over Eastleigh, Hampshire, aged thirty-six years.

Born: Lingwood, Norfolk, 13.07.1918
(d. 02.01.2004)

Matches: 322

Batting:

Runs	HS	Av	100s
14,730	167*	34.7	24

Bowling:

Wkts	Av	BB
2	99.5	1-19

Catches: 320

Most of the players in the Lancashire sides of the 1950s will tell you that Geoff Edrich was one of Lancashire's best captains. In 1956 he skippered the First XI when Cyril Washbrook was playing for England and never lost a match. He captained the Second XI later with much success, spending the time bringing on young players like Geoff Pullar, Jack Bond and Tommy Greenhough.

Edrich arrived at Old Trafford after the war, during which he had suffered under the cruel heat and unmerciful rule of the Japanese for three and a half years, weighing just over six stone. It took him a year in the Norfolk air and his wife's cooking to recover his strength. Coach Harry Makepeace took Geoff under his wing in 1946 and after six matches he was awarded his county cap.

A man of strong principles, he showed relentless courage when batting. In his second season he made his maiden century at Blackpool against Warwickshire and went on to score 1,000 runs that year and did so for another seven seasons. In the early 1950s he scored over 2,000 in a season, outscoring Cyril Washbrook. In 1954 he made his highest individual total at Trent Bridge, 167 not out, the only century in the game. The following year

he was awarded a benefit against Derbyshire at Old Trafford and was presented with £3,375 which would have bought him a good-sized house at that time.

Chosen to tour with a strong Commonwealth team in 1953-54 Geoff Edrich played in three unofficial Test matches. He scored 2 centuries and averaged 40 on the tour. In his career he scored 15,600 runs including 26 centuries and took 330 catches as an expert fielder. He is the only captain to have won a game without losing a wicket in either innings. Another special occasion arrived when he scored a century against Middlesex, who were captained by his brother Bill.

In those days committees believed that players should be servile and Edrich was wrongly dismissed. He left to play cricket in Cumberland and worked as a labourer in a steelworks in the winter, so much injustice and little respect for his important contribution to the war effort and the world of cricket. In 1962 he was appointed coach and head groundsman at the attractive Cheltenham College ground, where he stayed until his retirement. Later he underwent radiography for cancer and his indomitable fighting spirit brought him through. The Lancashire Players' Association voted him as their President and the club awarded him a Vice-Presidency in 2000. He kept his strong links with the club until his death in 2004.

Farokh Engineer
RHB & WK, 1968-76

Born: Bombay, 25.02.1938

Matches: 175

Batting:

Runs	HS	Av	100s
5,942	141	26.6	4

Catches: 429

Stumpings: 35

Tests: 46

A natural athlete, Farokh Engineer was a most flamboyant wicketkeeper, whose presence in the side enabled Lancashire to succeed in winning many trophies. He was born for limited-overs cricket and added to his reputation by opening the batting with dashing displays which brought early boundaries and an invaluable start to the game.

Farokh was born in Bombay in 1938, the son of Parsee parents. He was thirty years old and an experienced Indian Test player when he joined Lancashire in 1968. As the most experienced cricketer in the side he gave it some balance and an essential ingredient.

A most positive and dominant personality behind the stumps, he was India's first-choice wicketkeeper for fifteen years, making his debut for his national side in 1961. A brilliant wicketkeeper, he was fairly tall and broad with huge hands. Consistently alert with swift movement, he lifted his side's confidence and less gifted bowlers became triumphant. Standing close to the stumps for the fast men, he was rewarded with records that still hold. He had 8 dismissals in a match four times. In the 1970 season, he claimed 91 victims, a total seldom dreamed of by most wicketkeepers in that period.

Exciting to watch, he side-skipped down the pitch to hit a full toss from the meat of the bat. Sometimes erratic in performance, the spectators were always given their money's worth, in front or behind the wickets. He brought in the crowds, so many that thousands were locked out at Southport in 1969 when he hammered the Glamorgan bowling to annihilate the opposition in the first season of Sunday League cricket. In a Roses game at Sheffield he hit a magnificent 96 and tried to reach his century in dramatic fashion with a six – and was caught, choosing to entertain his way. He scored nearly 3,000 runs in 152 one-day innings and added 183 dismissals as wicketkeeper in his usual spectacular and entertaining style. His first-class contribution was almost 6,000 runs averaging 26 with 4 centuries. In all first-class cricket he made well over 13,000 runs and scored centuries all round the world.

On a secret trip to India with the Lancashire team, many years after retirement, he was welcomed with the reverence of a rajah by crowds, opening doors for us all to visit where we wished.

There is something of the talisman about Farokh. Endless stories abound about his benefit year when he more than doubled previous amounts. He was unique, an unforgettable Lancastrian who still runs his textile firm in close proximity to his county's headquarters. He enriches the Old Trafford family with his regular visits and was made a Vice-President in 2004.

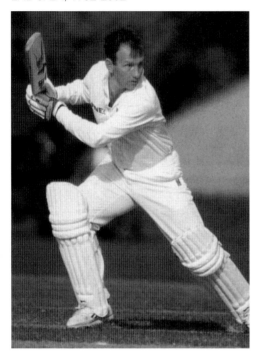

Born: Warrington, 09.09.1963

Matches: 337

Batting:

Runs	HS	Av	100s
19,603	366	42.4	47

Bowling:

Wkts	Av	BB
7	70	2-91

Catches: 273

Tests: 10

Eighteen-year-old Neil Fairbrother was picked to play for his league side Grappenhall when he received an early phone call from Jack Bond to join the Lancashire first team against Kent at Old Trafford. The match was rain-affected, but he did walk out to field behind the captain Clive Lloyd. Mike Watkinson was another youthful Second XI player to be selected and they were the last amateurs to turn out for a Lancashire team in a first-class match.

Neil Harvey Fairbrother was named after the great Australian left-hander, his mother's favourite cricketer. How she knew her son would be left-handed or turn out to be one of Lancashire's most famous sons is a mystery. His father and two uncles played league cricket but 'Harvey' was a bit special. Called up to play for England Young Cricketers against Australia, he scored 90 runs in the mini-Test at Chelmsford, looking the best player among the English batsman.

In his first Lancashire first-class innings at Edgbaston, Harvey was only 6 runs short of his century when an arranged declaration came. There was no complaint from this talented young cricketer, who went on to score another seven half-centuries in his first season

and finished fourth in the Lancashire batting averages.

Scoring 1,000 runs the following summer, a feat he performed in ten seasons, he scored his maiden century against Derbyshire at Buxton. Harvey was top scorer in Lancashire's Benson & Hedges Cup-winning side at Lord's in 1984. The following summer he was the only Lancastrian to score 1,000 runs; this included a century in each of the Roses games.

Harvey was a most entertaining left-hand batsman, quick on his feet playing from back or front foot. At 5ft 8ins he was often compared with the brilliant Eddie Paynter and the two remain the only Lancastrians to score 300 runs in a day. Harvey had a most powerful drive, often clearing the field. He could hook and pull magnificently and play fast or slow bowling equally well. The opposition found it difficult to set a field because he was the best placer of the ball in the game, always finding the gaps, often with a little improvisation. The scoreboard ticked along from his first ball and he became valued as a one-day player where quick runs were at a premium. But Harvey was a great Lancashire batsman in all forums of cricket. He scored more first-class runs for his county than any other player in the last forty years as well as more runs in the limited-overs games than any other Lancashire batsman. Courageous and aggressive at the crease, he was a winner, a formidable opponent, batting at No.4 in all types of cricket.

It is generally agreed that his 10 Test match appearances were too few but lack of chances has happened to many excellent batsmen before him. Harvey played 75 one-day international matches for England from 1986 to 1999 including 3 World Cup tournaments. He appeared in ten domestic one-day finals at Lord's for Lancashire. Only one other player has equalled that record, Underwood of Kent. No player achieved more than his 16 gold awards for his county.

1,000 first-class runs in May has been achieved by only three players in the history of the game: W.G. Grace, Wally Hammond and Lancashire's Charlie Hallows. Harvey reached 1,000 runs in all competitions in May 1990 and topped the first-class batting with an average of 85. He was an important team member of the Lancashire side to win both domestic cup finals at Lord's that year, the first county to do so. In a match against Surrey at The Oval that same year, he scored a century before lunch, another before tea and a third before close of play, being finally dismissed for 366 the following day. It was the third highest individual score in first-class cricket. The partnership of 364 with Atherton is still a 3rd wicket record for Lancashire. The following season, continuing his rich vein of form, he scored a century in the one-day international against the West Indies, winning another gold award for Man of the Match. His partnership of 213 with Hick was a record for any wicket in one-day internationals in England.

During 1992 and 1993, his two years as captain of Lancashire, Harvey's determination, enthusiasm and winning attitude was evident in a Benson & Hedges Cup-tie with Surrey at The Oval. He played a captain's innings of 87, driving and pulling a strong bowling attack and holding the side together to reach a total of 236. Surrey started with a record partnership of 212, only 24 runs behind with 9 wickets left and a comfortable 6 overs. The last 9 Surrey wickets were captured for 18 runs, Harvey encouraging his team and changing his bowlers to clinch an astonishing victory. The gold award went to the irrepressible Lancashire captain who went on to take his side to the final at Lord's.

Another domestic cup double came in 1996 after winning the Benson & Hedges Cup the previous season. More limited-overs titles arrived in 1998 with the NatWest Trophy win at Lord's and the National League title which was won again the following season. Into the new millennium and Harvey was still topping the Lancashire batting: in his penultimate season he averaged 62.

A magnificent fielder, particularly in the covers and later at slip, Harvey could turn his arm on occasions with his gentle left-arm medium pace. He took only 7 first-class wickets in 20 seasons but all his victims were top batsmen, and 5 were Test players in their prime. The surprising list includes Richard Hadlee, Clive Rice, Tim Curtis, John Morris and Ronnie Irani, and the other two were captains of their counties, John Barclay and David Bias.

For 20 seasons Neil Fairbrother has been at the heart of Lancashire cricket. He has scored over 20,000 runs in first-class cricket with 47 centuries, one against every county except Kent. He was a consistent run-scorer, a reliable general in the side for two decades. A massive record benefit of over £200,000 reflected the huge appreciation the Lancashire public had for Neil Fairbrother, a favourite and loyal son of Lancashire County Cricket.

Born: Westhoughton, 23.05.1903

(d. 15.11.1979)

Matches: 134

Batting:

Runs	HS	Av
2,202	63	21.1

Catches: 232

Stumpings: 65

Tests: 4

A wicketkeeping world record was broken in 1930 when Bill Farrimond made 7 dismissals in an innings against Kent at Old Trafford. Bill was an excellent keeper, particularly neat on close-to-the-wicket skills. He was technically proficient, undemonstrative and unpretentious in character. He was a down-to-earth Westhoughton lad, where he was born, bred, married and buried. He lived for many years in the semi-detached house adjoining that of his friend Dick Pollard. Bill was popular, well-respected and possessed of a dry sense of humour. He treated the softer, cravatted amateurs as if they were pros, never allowing them an easy game. Bill's career ran parallel with that of George Duckworth, who claimed the first team place. Bill played in the Second XI most of his career, and he was accomplished enough to play 4 Test matches for England, twice against South Africa in 1931 when Duckworth was ill, once against the West Indies in 1935 and again against the South Africans the same year at Lord's. On the last two occasions, Les Ames was playing as a batsman and outfielder.

Bill was a better batsman than Duckworth. He scored heavily for the Second XI and, given more opportunity with the first team, he could have batted regularly in the top six. His highest score in first-class cricket was an excellent 174 for the Minor Counties in 1934. He played only one match that year for a strong Lancashire side, scoring an unbeaten 61. The following year he averaged over 30 in the season for the First XI. In the latter part of his career he continued to score runs and in 1939, playing regularly after Duckworth's retirement, he opened with the captain, Lionel Lister, against Surrey at Old Trafford, top scoring in the first innings with 55. He went on to score 50 at Cardiff and 63 at Gloucester, making well over 500 runs in the season with a benefit match against Middlesex before the war stopped all cricket.

Bill refused offers earlier in his career to qualify for other counties, the majority of which would have been delighted to add a top-class keeper to their side. A patient and loyal man with a comfortable social life, he was content to receive less remuneration and play alongside his mates in the second team. His most impressive CV with England and Lancashire Seconds seemed to satisfy his needs as long as he could continue to live in Westhoughton.

Claiming 297 victims in first-class cricket and hundreds more in his Second XI career, Bill returned to his Westhoughton league side to win the Bolton League Championship four years on the run. He died aged seventy-six years and, just before his death in 1979, he told me he wouldn't have changed anything if given the chance. Being able to play the game he loved among his Lancashire friends was all he wished.

Andrew Flintoff

RHB & RMF, 1995-present

Born: Preston, 03.12.1977

Matches: 65

Batting:

Runs	HS	Av	100s
3,488	160	37.1	9

Bowling:

Wkts	Av	BB
63	31.1	5-24

Catches: 90

Tests: 29

Representing Lancashire and England Youth teams, Andrew was always in demand twelve months in the year; he was over-bowled at youth level and began to suffer back problems.

He made his first-class debut at Portsmouth against Hampshire at seventeen years of age. In the first three years 'Freddie's' 6ft 4ins physique was protected and his bowling arm rested. His batting developed and he made his maiden century when nineteen years old against Hampshire at Southampton.

At twenty years his confidence and aggressive style was evident from early season. He hit 61 from 24 balls against the quick and well-respected Alex Tudor of Surrey at Old Trafford. As expected, he fitted into the one-day side with ease and played his part in Lancashire winning the NatWest Trophy and the National League competition in 1998. Freddie topped the England 'A' team averages on the tour to Zimbabwe and South Africa with an average of 77. Beginning to contribute to the bowling attack, he took 4 for 22 for England 'A' against Zimbabwe 'A' demonstrating his all-round ability. On his one-day international debut for England at Sharjah against Pakistan he scored a quick half-century which included 4 sixes.

Many memorable innings followed, with inspired onslaughts and powerful displays from the crease. In the National League, Freddie smashed the Essex attack for 143 from 66 balls at Chelmsford. Eighty per cent of his score was made from boundaries, including 9 sixes. After

representing his county in the World Cup, Freddie joined Lancashire at Bristol and cracked the fastest century of the season before lunch, the last 50 runs coming from only 18 balls. Following that game – an innings of enormous power, driving, cutting and pulling – he topped his best score with 160 against Yorkshire in the Roses game at Old Trafford. Scoring a century before lunch, he became the first Lancastrian to do so in a Roses match.

Remodelling his stance in 2000 to a more upright position to assist his back recovery, Freddie continued to entertain and win six Man of the Match awards in the next two years. One of these highlights included a memorable unbeaten 135 from 111 balls in the quarter finals against Surrey at The Oval. Another was a gold award for his fast and accurate bowling in a one-day international against New Zealand, taking 4 for 17.

His maiden Test century came at Christchurch in 2002. With savage blows and powerful straight drives he shared a partnership with Thorpe of 281, the best England partnership for any wicket in New Zealand.

Into the record books already, there is no doubt Freddie will continue to hit the headlines and empty bars around the world. In these early days he has scored almost 5,000 first-class runs and taken over 100 first-class wickets, almost matching this record in one-day cricket. Great characters are essential to attract the crowds to follow the game. Freddie is for the future, a great entertainer in all forms of cricket.

Graeme Fowler

LHB & RM (& occas. WK), 1979-92

Born: Accrington, 20.04.1957

Matches: 234

Batting:

Runs	HS	Av	100s
13,453	226	36.5	29

Bowling:

Wkts	Av	BB
8	39	2-34

Catches: 126

Stumpings: 5

Tests: 21

Life was too short not to enjoy every single moment and 'Foxy' Fowler strove to achieve his aspirations. He believed his major role as a professional cricketer was to entertain. His extrovert, infectious enthusiasm invaded the field of play and dressing rooms all over the world. A man of practical jokes, he believed his impish humour would break down the intensity of the game, relax colleagues and improve performances and team spirit. Underneath the humorous banter was an obvious passion for the game and a dedicated, ambitious player.

An aggressive and brave left-handed batsman, he possessed a sharp eye, essential for an adventurous cricketer. Displaying a flourish of off-side hard-hitting cuts and drives, the scoreboard ticked over quickly when Foxy was batting. England Schoolboys witnessed his early talents as a wicketkeeper batsman. After qualifying as a P.E. teacher at Durham University, he made his Lancashire debut against Derbyshire at twenty-two years and was seen scoring 1,000 runs a season in the 1980s. The outcome of this success resulted in his meteoric excursion into Test cricket. One outstanding innings was the century at Lord's against the West Indies, arguably as good an attack as any Test bowling side this century. This was his second Test century, his first was against Pakistan at The Oval the previous year. His most notable Test innings in statistical terms was the magnificent double century in Madras, batting for 565 minutes in soaring temperatures.

A record 10 consecutive sixes in a whirlwind century of 46 minutes for his county against Leicestershire was the kind of explosive performance members witnessed. Admittedly irregular bowlers were used, but extraordinary energy and power was demonstrated. The previous season he scored a century in each innings against Warwickshire in an astonishing match of broken records. Hurt while fielding on the first day, Foxy scored a century in each innings with a runner to win the game.

Scoring almost 12,000 first-class runs, he was also a prolific scorer in the limited-overs game with nearly 7,000 more. Playing in 21 Tests and 26 one-day internationals, winning gold awards and breaking Lancashire records in all types of cricket, he earns his place among Lancashire's 100 Greats. A brilliant fielder, first in the covers and then at slip, he showed his great athleticism in any position.

Music was always an equal love to his chosen sport. His timing and hand and feet coordination were transferred to the drums and he yearned to play in a rock band. He owned a colourful, varied wardrobe and drove a well travelled E-type Jaguar. Being a part-time model, raconteur, impressionist, author and perceptive commentator were other experiences. His successful benefit was proof of the popularity of this irrepressibly cheerful character who could never be ignored.

Born: Liverpool, 19.11.1879 (d. 03.12.1917)

Matches: 144

Batting:

Runs	HS	Av	100s
5,599	139	26.1	5

Bowling:

Wkts	Av	BB
8	28	2-18

Catches: 174

Stumpings: 14

At the turn of the century, Harold Garnett was batting so magnificently that he seemed likely to become the best left-handed amateur batsman in England. He was widely admired for his attractive, classical style of play and his forceful hitting. Opening the innings with Archie MacLaren in his first full season, he scored centuries against Sussex, Middlesex and Leicester with half a dozen innings just short of a century. His season's total of 1,689 runs was second only to J.T. Tyldesley. The Liverpool-born amateur made a dramatic entrance on the cricketing stage.

MacLaren's influence as captain of England was crucial in taking Garnett to Australia in the winter. His spectacular form justified a place on the tour joining three other Lancastrians. As a competent keeper he would be cover for Lilley. Alas, he lost form completely, averaging only single figures, and was never chosen for a Test match.

On his return to Lancashire his form improved. In 1903 he played a magnificent innings against Yorkshire opening with Reggie Spooner: he scored 122 against the best of Yorkshire's bowlers, Hirst, Rhodes, F.S. Jackson and Haigh. Lancashire's side was dominated by amateurs with only three professionals. At Bristol on a rain-affected pitch Garnett, in a short spell, took 2 for 18 with his slow left-arm spin.

The following year the side were undefeated and won the Championship. Garnett, though never spectacular in this period, batted steadily and made his contribution to the side's success.

Like most of the amateurs, his work took preference and his business took him to other parts of the world, mainly Argentina where he continued to play club cricket. The country has a network of fine club sides and some engaging English county cricketers to coach or play. After five years away he returned for the 1911 season, finding a place in the county side for 24 matches and helping in the wicketkeeping department, batting further down the order.

Business took him away for the following two seasons and in 1914, he scored an unbeaten century in two hours at Trent Bridge. It was his nimble proficiency behind the stumps that had been honed in his club cricket abroad and this was recognised by a call to play for the Gentlemen v. Players at Lord's. He made four dismissals; one which particularly made the headlines in the press was the magnificent stumping of Bill Hitch who had begun to develop a good partnership. The match was won, Garnett proving his all-round ability at the highest level.

At the outbreak of war, Harold Garnett volunteered for service. Given the commission of captain, he was killed in action on the Italian front aged thirty-eight.

David Green
RHB & OB, 1959-67

Born: Caernarfon, 10.11.1939

Matches: 135

Batting:

Runs	HS	Av	100s
6,086	138	26.2	4

Bowling:

Wkts	Av	BB
41	45	3-6

Catches: 40

A well-built opening batsman, the name of David Green is popular in quiz questions as the only man to have reached 2,000 first-class runs in a season without scoring a century. He achieved this in 1965 with a highest score of 85 against Warwickshire. The consistently good scores throughout that season when he shared several prolific opening partnerships with Geoff Pullar took him to the top of the Lancashire batting averages.

He was born in Llanengan, North Wales, because his mother temporarily escaped the expected bombing of Manchester at the outbreak of war. Educated at Manchester Grammar School, he headed their batting averages and appeared for the Public Schools at Lord's. Playing for Bowden in the Manchester Association and Lancashire Seconds he entered Oxford University to read history in 1959. When Lancashire visited The Parks, Greeny scored 50 for Oxford and dismissed Wharton, Pullar and Dyson as an occasional off-break bowler. Showing good technique and patience, he was soon opening the innings with his captain, A.C. Smith, later of Warwickshire and England, and made his maiden century at The Parks against Middlesex. It was at Oxford that he bowled his most successful spell, 5 for 61 at Hove. Greeny went on to earn blues in 3 consecutive years.

Making his debut for Lancashire at Southampton at nineteen years of age, he joined some illustrious and experienced players in Washbrook, Grieves and Wharton. He scored 1,000 first-class runs that season and continued his occasional off-break bowling taking 3 wickets for 6 runs at Leicester. In his final year at Oxford, joining the Lancashire squad later in the season, he scored his first county century against Northamptonshire. Playing as an amateur he was capped in 1962.

The following year he tried to establish himself in business. In the winter he played rugby for Sale where he met Lancashire secretary Geoffrey Howard, who suggested that he sign professional terms for Lancashire Cricket Club and the following year repeated his good form with 1,000 runs.

Due to injuries and illness and after missing most of the 1967 season, Greeny decided to make a fresh start at Gloucestershire. It worked well for a season, when he again reached 2,000 runs, with his highest career score of 233 at Hove. In his fourth and final season there he batted for Gloucestershire in that famous Gillette Cup game at Old Trafford that went on until almost nine o'clock in the evening. A tour of Rhodesia with the International Wanderers capped his playing career in which he reached a total of 13,381 runs.

After twelve years with a contract catering company he became a successful sports writer and author.

Leonard Green
RHB, 1922-35

Born: Whalley, 01.02.1890 (d. 02.03.1963)

Matches: 152

Batting:

Runs	HS	Av	100s
3,575	110*	24.6	1

Bowling:

Wkts	Av	BB
9	33.2	2-2

Catches: 36

As captain of Lancashire from 1926 to 1928, Leonard Green can claim the best record as leader. He won a hat-trick of championships. Many believe the side in the last year of the three was Lancashire's best. Success depends on good leadership and this was Major Green's great strength. He joined the East Lancashire Regiment serving in the First World War, where he earned the Military Cross.

Green was a prominent batsman at his local club, Whalley, near Blackburn. He played for Lancashire in 1922 and the following season scored an undefeated century against Gloucestershire to help win the game. At thirty-six years of age he was invited to captain the county side, the Committee believing his leadership qualities would bring success. It was an enlightened move. Major Green was a disciplinarian who excelled at man management. The Lancashire team of that time was made up of experienced players, most of whom were strong characters and opinionated about the game. Major Green, in comparison, was tactically inexperienced (and rather aptly named), but he understood players. He could draw the best out of the ordinary and he united a group of individuals into a hungry team. He was the least gifted member and leant on senior professionals for advice. The opening batsmen were Harry Makepeace (who wouldn't suffer fools gladly) and the experienced Charlie Hallows (who was to become one of the leading coaches in the game). The prolific Ernest Tyldesley came in next, and he was to score more runs than any other player in the history of the county. In the side were the extroverted Duckworth, the rebellious Cec Parkin and the gifted Australian bowler McDonald. Leadership was crucial, and he honed together a unit working in perfect symbiosis. It was a team of talented cricketers of course, but without the hand on the rudder clear direction would not be guaranteed.

Major Green was a useful batsman, averaging over 30 in his best season as captain. He batted at No.7, was a reliable fielder and only rarely bowled his right-arm ordinary, taking 12 first-class wickets. He was invited to tour Jamaica with Tennyson's team in 1926-27 and three years later travelled with Sir Julien Cahn's team to Argentina. Scoring almost 4,000 first-class runs, he averaged over 25 in his career.

Achieving the rank of Colonel before retiring from the Army, Len Green served on the Lancashire Committee for many years, becoming President in 1951-52. He was an all-round sportsman, also playing hockey and rugby at county level. It was his qualities as captain that earned him the right to be among Lancashire's greats.

Born: Rochdale, 09.11.1931

Matches: 241

Batting:

Runs	HS	Av
1,868	76*	8.5

Bowling:

Wkts	Av	BB
707	21.9	7-56

Catches: 81

Tests: 4

Tom excelled at cricket when he was in short trousers. Among his memorabilia is a cricket ball presented to him for taking 85 wickets in a season for Fieldhouse Seconds at just fourteen years of age. At sixteen years he joined Lancashire but before he had made his first team appearance he fell 30ft from a loading bay at the printers yard where he worked in the winter. He smashed bones in both feet so badly that one foot was still out of shape when he retired. Seeing the injury, Lancashire refused to renew his contract but he persuaded the Committee to sign him on a week by week basis. Determined to succeed, Tom made his first-class debut in 1951 shortly after he broke his fingers playing in the leagues.

As well as those horrific injuries, Greenhough had to compete for his place with international spinners Malcolm Hilton, Roy Tattersall and Bob Berry. Five years after his debut he was awarded his county cap and was taken to Jamaica with the Duke of Norfolk's XI. Three years later he had become England's leading leg-break bowler, taking 122 wickets, and was called up to play for his country against India. In his second Test match at Lord's he took 5-35 in the first innings, some achieve-ment after being told he would never bowl again after those early injuries.

When umpires and players complained about his delivery action roughing up the pitch, Tom announced his temporary retire-ment from the game after just 2 Tests in order to remedy the fault. Correcting the problem, he received his deserved reward by being selected for the Fifth Test match at The Oval and for the MCC tour to the West Indies.

His excellent season in 1960 with 121 wick-ets at 18.2 brought him another Test call against the South Africans. He suffered further injuries to fingers and shoulders but always came back fighting. He produced his career best, 7 for 56 against the champion county, Worcestershire.

Tommy took 751 wickets in his career, play-ing in around half the games he might have done. Had he not fought against all odds, including preventing a surgeon from amputat-ing a finger following a cricket injury, he could never have achieved his ambition to play so well for county and country. Those who saw him will always remember that enthusiastic bouncy spring and hop in his run-up, expect-ing a wicket with every ball.

He overcame so many obstacles throughout his career that, unwittingly, he has inspired all Lancastrians to learn from his adaptability, persistence and self belief.

Ken Grieves

RHB & LBG, 1949-64

Born: Sydney, 27.08.1925 (d. 03.01.1992)

Matches: 452

Batting:

Runs	HS	Av	100s
20,802	224	33.9	26

Bowling:

Wkts	Av	BB
235	28.8	6-60

Catches: 556

One of a rare breed of players to score 20,000 runs for his adopted county after the Second World War, the multi-talented Grieves sailed past that total as well as taking 556 catches and 235 wickets for the county.

Arriving in England in 1947 from his native Australia, Ken Grieves was employed as Bury's goalkeeper in the winter and Rawtenstall's cricket professional in the summer. Ken was a natural ball player and a brilliant close-to-the-wicket catcher. He still holds a record for Lancashire with the most catches in a match as an outfielder, 8 against Sussex at Old Trafford in 1951.

An athletic, handsome figure, often capless, he looked tall because of his upright stance. He nurtured his most effective shot off the back foot, scoring square into the covers or executing a delicate late cut to the boundary. In only his second match he scored a total of 159 in 2 innings with superb drives through the covers as well as taking 8 wickets, confirming his all-round ability. Two games later he scored the first of 26 centuries and completed 1,000 runs in his first season. He reached that target every season except two and in 1959 reached 2,000. Awarded his cap in June 1949, he showed his appreciation by taking 6 for 60 to beat Kent by an innings.

The first of his double centuries was against Cambridge University at Fenners in 1957. There was another double century made against them at Old Trafford and a third against the Indian tourists at Blackpool in 1959.

Although he was not a consistently accurate leg-spinner and googly bowler, he achieved quick wickets when conditions were suitable. He was relied upon as a change bowler who could break partnerships. His benefit match was interrupted by rain and his meagre £5,700 was never a fair recognition of his prodigious talent. Ken toured India with the Commonwealth XI in 1950-51 scoring 1,000 runs on the tour, averaging over 40 and playing in all 5 'unofficial Tests'. He was praised in dispatches for his brilliant slip fielding. Ken Grieves was good enough to be picked for any Test side in his day with perhaps the exception of the 1948 Australians.

As well as a gifted all-rounder at cricket, Ken was a competent golfer and an excellent goalkeeper for Bolton Wanderers and Stockport County as well as Bury. He served on the Lancashire Committee for thirteen years and was respected by his colleagues as a most popular member. Elected a Vice-President of the club in December 1991, he died three weeks later after enjoying a round of golf.

Charlie Hallows

LHB & SLA, 1914-32

Born: Little Lever, 04.04.1895 (d. 10.11.1972)

Matches: 370

Batting:

Runs	HS	Av	100s
20,142	233*	39.7	52

Bowling:

Wkts	Av	BB
19	41.2	3-28

Catches: 135

Tests: 2

Lancashire's team in the mid-1920s headed the Championship table in three successive years. In 1928 they were unbeaten mainly because of the superb balance of the team, who were at the top of their form. Many believe this team was the best of all Lancashire sides.

Charlie Hallows was an opening batsman, left-handed and an entertaining stroke player. Tall, dark and handsome, he had a full head of hair even in his later years and always appeared well groomed. His slim figure and enthusiastic nature never changed throughout his long cricketing career.

His flamboyant and rhythmical start to the 1928 season brought him 4 centuries in May and with only two days left he needed 232 runs to achieve 1,000 runs in that first month. The Sussex attack at Old Trafford included the formidable England bowling partnership of Maurice Tate and Arthur Gilligan. At the end of the first day's play Hallows had entertained majestically with 190 not out and crowds came in to the ground the following day to witness an astonishing landmark. At the vital run he was almost caught at square leg, such was his nervous state, but he made it. After a congratulatory celebration on the field by all players, Hallows was out next ball.

1,000 runs in May has only been achieved by three cricketers, the lordly W.G. Grace, the great Wally Hammond and our own Charlie Hallows. The Lancashire player had the best average of the three that year.

This stylish batsman scored over 20,000 runs for his county including over 50 centuries, 11 of them in 1928. His career average with Lancashire was over 40. It was reported in the press that he hit one ball into the railway station. Spectators rumoured that it had entered a goods wagon and finished up in Birmingham. His opening partner was the cautious Harry Makepeace who was a perfect foil for the more attractive left-hander. As openers, Makepeace and Hallows were household names, like Hornby and Barlow or Washbrook and Place later. Hobbs and Sutcliffe were so established in the England starting line up that Hallows only played 2 Test matches for his country, one against the strong 1921 Australians. The second was against the West Indies six years later when Hobbs was injured. In other times he would have been a regular England opener.

Retiring from county cricket in the early 1930s, he was employed as a league professional in clubs based in England, Scotland, Ireland and Wales. Still enthusiastic about the game, he was a good communicator and after five years as a coach for Worcestershire he returned home to Old Trafford to coach the players at a youthful seventy-four years of age.

Many will remember him for his merry month of May in 1928, but during his long career he gave stability to the Lancashire batting. An excellent fielder with a good cricket brain, he passed on his vast experience as a well-respected coach.

Jim Hallows

LHB & LFM, 1898-1907

Born: Little Lever, 14.11.1873 (d. 20.05.1910)

Matches: 138

Batting:

Runs	HS	Av	100s
4,997	137*	28.5	8

Bowling:

Wkts	Av	BB
279	23.6	9-37

Catches: 57

There were many shared similarities between James Hallows and Johnnie Briggs, though Jim reached fewer heights. Hallows was a left-arm spinner and batsman who suffered from epileptic fits. He experienced one while playing in a Roses game in 1905. Both died young and should have played longer. Jim was born in the industrial village of Little Lever in 1873, two miles from Bolton, and was the uncle of Charlie who was to follow him and play county cricket twice as long. Jim suffered poor health from youth and was advised to take outdoor exercise. He showed ability as an all-round cricketer and played for the local Temperance XI, moving up to Little Lever Cricket Club and heading their averages in his first year. A fragile figure, he overcame any physical weakness by his enthusiasm for the game. Invited to play in a Colt's match at Manchester in 1896, he created local headlines by scoring 133 and 77 not out. Old Trafford coaches witnessed this performance and invited him to play at the Lancashire headquarters the following season as a member of the ground staff.

Jim had been bowling fast but was advised by Sydney Crossfield to change his action to slow left-arm and vary his pace and flight. Crossfield was an influential amateur who had been joint captain with Archie MacLaren four years earlier. Jim made his Lancashire debut at Lord's against the MCC in 1898 as a middle-order left-hand batsman and first change bowler. By the turn of the century he was making 1,000 runs in the season but then fell back in form as his health suffered. Success depended on him being strong, and he recovered in 1904 to full health and top form.

As a batsman he made most of his runs on the off side with hard cuts and off drives. Gilbert Jessop said his shots were the hardest he ever had to field in the covers. Accompanied by a strong defence, Jim built an innings waiting patiently for bad balls. In this memorable season of 1904 he hit 3 centuries and shared a stand of 296 with Reggie Spooner. His bowling was slow to medium pace but full of spin and variety. Two outstanding bowling performances that year were at Gloucester taking 9 for 37 and at Aigburth against the same side with 8 for 50, 12 in the match.

On the last Championship game of the season in late August, Jim needed 15 runs to complete his double of 1,000 runs and 100 wickets. Seven Derbyshire bowlers tried to separate the hundred partnership with Spooner and, unable to do so, congratulated Jim on his deserved accomplishment. He was the first Lancashire-born player to achieve the double and a presentation was made to him after the game. Wisden recognised his qualities and chose him as one of their great cricketers of the season. Alas, it was his last healthy season and he died aged thirty-six.

Frank Hayes

RHB, 1970-84

Born: Preston, 06.12.1946

Matches: 228

Batting:

Runs	HS	Av	100s
10,899	187	37.4	22

Catches: 150

Tests: 9

Representing the Lancashire Federation and England Schoolboys in his early career, Frank took three years away studying for his science degree at Sheffield where he captained his university cricket team and represented the university at rugby and soccer. Joining Lancashire, he made an explosive impact with the Second XI in 1970, scoring an unbeaten double century at Edgbaston followed by a century in the return fixture. It enthused Warwickshire and England's Tom Dollery to announce him as the best stroke player he had ever seen and an England certainty. By midsummer he had made his first-class debut against Middlesex at Old Trafford scoring 94 and 47. In the next game at Southampton he was stumped on 99. Other high scores followed and he finished fourth in the county batting averages.

His maiden century came in 1973 at Hove, followed by others at Swansea and two at Old Trafford against Nottinghamshire and Somerset. England selectors admired his natural talent and Frank was called up that year to play his first Test match against the West Indies at The Oval. He scored a brilliant century in his debut game, the first Lancastrian to achieve it. An automatic choice for the tour of the Caribbean the following winter, he returned to record another 1,000 runs for his county. That included his highest score of 187 against the Indian tourists at Old Trafford.

An explosive hitter, Frank scored 119 at Swansea, sharing a partnership of over 200 with Barry Wood. He hit the Glamorgan bowler Nash for 5 sixes and a four in 1 over, almost equalling Gary Sobers' record of 6 sixes from the same bowler at the same venue nine years earlier. At the end of that season he recorded a Championship average of over 57. The following year he was elected captain of his county for three years and in each of those years maintained second place in the county averages to Clive Lloyd.

A handsome, athletic figure, Frank possessed a natural talent. His timing of the ball was memorable. An elegant stroke player, he effused class with a great repertoire of strokes around the wicket. As a young cricketer he showed few weaknesses. He could hit the ball over extra cover as well as leg-side sixes. Particularly lusty against spin bowling, he hit the great Bishan Bedi high into the Old Trafford score box roof on the Stretford end. There was a fidgety nervousness about his style, patting his bat violently at the crease as the bowler approached, but the strokes were orthodox.

A brittle bone condition curtailed a brilliant talent. Injuries became more numerous and he retired in 1984 having played 9 Test matches, all against the West Indies, and totalling well over 13,000 first-class runs as well as almost 5,000 limited-overs runs.

He is honest, forthright in opinion, great company and always last to bed on a night out. The students at Felstead and Oakham school will be enriched by his presence.

Born: Burnley, 12.08.1882 (d. 30.01.1951)

Matches: 210

Batting:

Runs	HS	Av	100s
5,146	132no	18.9	1

Bowling:

Wkts	Av	BB
412	23	9-43

Catches: 76

On uncovered wickets, quality, accurate spinners were a vital ingredient in a balanced attack. In the early part of the century Lancashire had Bill Huddleston, Lol Cook and Jimmy Heap. The latter was a graceful, left-arm spinner who could be devastating on drying pitches. Accurate in line and length, he bowled a well-flighted ball to give extra bite. On slow pitches he turned the ball sharply away from the right-hander, enticing a false stroke as most of his victims were caught on the off side. His art of bowling included the deceptive ball that went straight on with the arm and after the First World War particularly, he achieved good figures.

Heap was called into the Lancashire side at twenty years of age to play against the touring Philadelphians at Old Trafford. Their great fast bowler Barton King took 9 for 62 in the second innings but the Lancashire debutant defended, stubbornly unbeaten on 38 while wickets around him tumbled. He showed his batting talent on many occasions, hitting an unbeaten century at Bournemouth against Hampshire just before the war. He was just short of 1,000 runs in 1913 when he also took 62 wickets, so the all-rounder tag could be applied to him with some justification.

It takes practice and experience to mature as a spin bowler and James Heap in his late twenties reaped the rewards of hard work despite his constant attacks of lumbago. At Northampton in 1910 he overwhelmed the home side, taking 9 for 43 (14 wickets in the match) to give Lancashire victory by an innings and 112 runs. In the same year he destroyed Gloucestershire at Old Trafford. In 13 overs he bowled 7 maidens and captured 5 for 16.

Heap was reaching his peak when war came. At Old Trafford he bowled 10 overs against Yorkshire's first innings, taking 6 for 16. None of the Yorkshire batsmen showed any confidence facing him and in the second innings he bowled out 5 for 23 to bring victory to his county by an innings. In the return match at Headingley he was top scorer with 90, unfortunately run out. The war years halted his developing career but he continued after a five-year break with 62 wickets in the season, including 14 in the match at Bristol. In the first innings he captured 7 for 27 in a remarkable spell. Well over 400 wickets and 5,000 runs for his county earned him a benefit of £1,804 in his last season. He carried on giving advice as a coach at Shrewsbury School.

Warren Hegg

RHB & WK, 1986-present

Born: Whitefield, 23.02.1968

Matches: 310

Batting:

Runs	HS	Av	100s
10,113	134	28	7

Catches: 762

Stumpings: 84

Tests: 2

Warren Hegg possessed unquenchable energy and enthusiasm combined with a controlled temperament. His ability to read the game well and positively encourage his colleagues makes him a perfect team man. A naturally talented wicketkeeper, he has shown exceptional glove work, particularly standing back.

As a junior at Stand Cricket Club, a perceptive coach saw him lacking concentration in the field and asked him to put on the keeper's gloves. He played for his club's first team at fourteen years before moving to the Bolton League side Tonge where he was tested against stronger opposition. Concurrently moving through the youth teams with Lancashire, 'Chucky' was a member of the Under-16 team which won the inter-county trophy beating Warwickshire in the final. Called up for the Under-19 England side when he was sixteen, he experienced international tournaments abroad.

Making his first-class debut for Lancashire at eighteen years at Lytham, he became the youngest wicketkeeper to score a first-class century in his second season. Two years later in a match against Derbyshire on a fast wicket at Chesterfield, Chucky took 11 catches; leaping, diving, pouncing, he equalled the world record for dismissals in a match. Eight years later he caught 10 of Yorkshire's batsmen in a Roses game at Headingley.

Chosen for three England 'A' tours, he played in Pakistan and Sri Lanka in 1990, the West Indies in 1994 and Australia in 1996. In 1993 he was called up to tour the West Indies

but suffered a bout of glandular fever which put his career back a couple of years. The deserved full England cap came when he made his Test match debut against Australia in the Boxing Day Ashes Test at the mighty Melbourne cricket ground. His uninhibited batting style has entertained memorably with numerous valuable innings. The one-day success with Lancashire has given him seven one-day finals at Lord's in a big-match atmosphere. He was awarded Man of the Match in one of the best ever limited-overs matches. Almost 100 runs were required from only 10 overs against Yorkshire in the semi-final of the Benson & Hedges Trophy when Warren cracked a magnificent 81, mostly off-side cuts and drives, that turned a lost game into a victory from the last ball. In first-class cricket Chucky has contributed admirably with runs, including 4 centuries. In 1990 he averaged over 40, fifth in the averages.

Success has not changed him. He passed George Duckworth's record number of 364 catches in September 2000 to set up a new record for his county. Taken out to India and New Zealand in 2001-02 he was kept in reserve, the management persisting with the inexperienced Foster. Always showing great dignity and integrity, Warren uttered no protest but advised and encouraged his younger colleague, giving him all his experience and help. Held in such high esteem as a player and a leader, Warren was appointed captain of Lancashire in 2002.

Ken Higgs

LHB & RFM, 1958-69

Born: Kidsgrove, 14.01.1937

Matches: 306

Batting:

Runs	HS	Av
2,655	60	10.9

Bowling:

Wkts	Av	BB
1,033	22.9	7-19

Catches: 155

Tests: 15

Few bowlers moved the ball from the pitch more consistently and accurately than Ken Higgs. His record proves his effectiveness on all kinds of pitches and he was able to earn his place in a first-class side until he was almost fifty years of age. Ken was a strongly built right-arm medium-fast bowler whose main asset was accuracy in line and length.

At school in Kidsgrove, Staffordshire, Higgs developed his all-round sporting ability, playing football for the school, his local Potteries team and eventually proving skilful enough to play centre half for Port Vale. But cricket was his first love and after a season with Staffordshire he signed for Lancashire. His Championship debut in 1958 was quite sensational. Opening the bowling with Brian Statham, he took 7 Hampshire wickets for 36 runs. The two bowled unchanged to win the match. He was to better that analysis with 7 for 19 against Leicestershire in 1965.

The counties played 28 Championship games before one-day cricket was introduced. When that competition came along Higgs was just as effective, taking over 50 wickets averaging just over 18 in the Gillette Cup alone.

Ken Higgs' best season was 1960, when he took 110 wickets at an average of 20. It was the season of his first Championship hat-trick against Essex at Blackpool on a pitch favouring the bat. Taking 5 wickets in 5 overs for 6 runs, he changed the complexion of the match. A further 2 hat-tricks were captured, against Yorkshire at Headingley and against

Hampshire when he was playing for Leicestershire. There was a fourth hat-trick in the 1974 Benson & Hedges Cup final for the Midlands county.

After representing Lancashire for over 300 games and taking 100 wickets in a season 5 times, he retired from first-class cricket for two years, playing for Rishton in the Lancashire leagues. Leicestershire spotted the unutilised talent and signed him in 1972.

Higgs' consistency was rewarded with a debut for England in 1965, and in less than three years he took 71 wickets in 15 Test matches. His most notable spell was 6 for 91 at Lord's against Gary Sobers' West Indies side in 1966. In the same series, steady batting saw him pick up a Test record 128 partnership for the last wicket with John Snow.

It was a stubborn resolve and endeavour that marked Ken Higgs' bowling, testing batsmen's patience with long spells of Pollard-like workmanship. Although a straight bat made him a useful tail-ender in first-class cricket and his large hands took over 300 catches, it was his valuable support as opening partner to Brian Stadham that cricket supporters will remember most. It is a pity his benefit year was held in the low-key period of fundraising in 1968 with a total of £8,390 – he would surely have been a minimum £100,000-man in today's more businesslike events. With over 1,000 wickets for Lancashire and 1,531 in all first-class cricket, he is Lancashire's fourth-highest wicket-taker in all cricket.

Malcolm Hilton

RHB & SLA, 1946-61

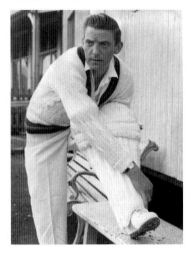

Born: Chadderton, 02.08.1928 (d. 08.07.1990)

Matches: 241

Batting:

Runs	HS	Av	100s
3,140	100*	12.1	1

Bowling:

Wkts	Av	BB
926	18.8	8-19

Catches: 187

Tests: 4

Playing for Lancashire at nineteen years of age against the Australian tourists at Old Trafford, Malcolm Hilton dismissed the mighty Don Bradman twice. He is still known for that match, which was only his third first-class game. The cricket world spoke of him, so great was Bradman's reputation.

A slim-framed, fair-haired figure with a distinctive sense of humour, Malcolm bowled left-arm spin at a brisk pace. He relied on turn rather than variety of pace or flight and was much less effective on dry pitches suiting the batsman. In conditions wet and drying, watchful crouchers surrounded the bat with spider-like hands, wanting to grasp the clicked ball in their web. The sharp spin and pace was very effective on uncovered wickets that had caught the showers.

The Bradman episode made his name, but it took a couple of years for him to achieve his first 100 wickets in the 1950 season. One outstanding performance was against Sussex in July at Old Trafford when he took 11 wickets for 50 runs in the match which was over in one day, the extra time being claimed to finish the game. 30 wickets fell in one day for 391 runs and conditions being in favour of the spinner, Hilton took 5 for 18 to dismiss Sussex for 51 in the late afternoon. That magnificent performance was followed by others, including 10 in the match against Middlesex and 9 in matches against Glamorgan home and away.

Opening the attack with Brian Statham on occasions, his success in 1950 helped to bring

the Championship to Lancashire, who shared it with Surrey. Quality spinners surface rarely and the selectors were nudged to select Malcolm for the final Test against the West Indies at The Oval. His season's performances the following year earned him another Test call against the South Africans at Headingley. The following winter he toured India with the MCC and in his one Test when conditions suited he took match figures of 9 for 93 to help win the game.

1956 was a memorable year for Malcolm, who achieved third place in the national averages with 158 wickets at less than 14. I saw the game at Weston-Super-Mare when he took 14 wickets in the match and his younger brother, who had moved down to Somerset, took 8 for the opposition. At the end of the season, playing for the Rest against Surrey, the champion county, he spun the ball viciously from leg in helpful conditions taking 6 wickets for 10 runs. His best bowling came two seasons on, when he claimed 8 wickets for 19 runs against the New Zealand tourists.

Hilton occasionally lost control of his length and line and retired into the leagues in his mid-thirties. Always enjoying the game, he was rewarded with outstanding performances. He was an outstanding fielder and once hit an unbeaten century batting at No.9 at Northampton. Wisden rewarded him as one of their five in 1957 but it was the Bradman dismissals so early in his career that sticks in the mind.

Len Hopwood
RHB & SLA, 1923-39

Born: Newton Hyde, 30.10.1903 (d. 15.06.985)

Matches: 397

Batting:

Runs	HS	Av	100s
15,519	220	30	27

Bowling:

Wkts	Av	BB
672	22.1	9-33

Catches: 197

Tests: 2

Recorded as the only Lancashire player to achieve the 'double' (1,000 runs and 100 wickets in a season) twice, Len was a stern right-handed batsman and an accurate left-arm slow bowler. He was not the most inspirational batsman to watch but he did a job, sometimes vital in saving or winning a match. There was very little backlift to his strokes, but they were effective. Appearing to the opposition to be a good handyman, he was a deceptive batsman, unyielding, collecting runs patiently, dispassionately, watchful and imperturbable at the crease.

Len bowled unceasingly by the hour, his left-arm spin accurate in length and curved flight. On damp wickets there was a vicious and quickening spin. Twice he took 9 wickets in an innings and 15 in the match. Bowling over the wicket there were sometimes six men on the leg side and he was rarely extravagant.

Len made his maiden century against the South African tourists at Liverpool in his second season of first-class cricket. Progress was slow and he served a long apprenticeship, including a two-season break in the mid-1920s playing for Wallasey and Cheshire. Returning for the 1928 Championship year he scored a couple of good centuries and took 43 wickets. When the 1930 Championship was won he had contributed 1,000 runs and taken 81 wickets.

Among his many accomplishments in the early 1930s he achieved a match double (a century and 10 wickets) against Leicestershire at Old Trafford. Another Championship title came in 1934 when Len's contribution was invaluable. He headed the bowling averages with 110 wickets at 17 runs each and scored over 1,500 runs averaging 41. Included in his magnificent season was an innings at Bristol when he scored 220, making a partnership of 316 with Ernest Tyldesley. Bowling over 1,000 overs, he took 7 for 13 against Glamorgan and captured 15 wickets in a match against Worcestershire at Blackpool. This season he achieved the first of his doubles in the Championship with a repeat the following year.

Len played 2 Test matches against Australia. At Old Trafford he bowled 47 overs and more than half were maidens, which kept Bradman quiet. As an opening batsman for Lancashire he went in No.8 for England without luck and was dismissed by Bill O'Reilly at Headingley and Manchester.

By shrewd and determined qualities he made himself into a player of good value. His chosen benefit match against Surrey was a disaster when rain interfered throughout the match. He received gate receipts of £138 but his expenses were £373. Donations came in from Lancashire supporters making £1,105. His overall contribution of 15,548 runs and 673 wickets had been appreciated. Len became the first professional player to be appointed President of Lancashire County Cricket Club in 1981/82.

A.H. Hornby
RHB, 1899-1914

Born: Nantwich, 29.7.1877 (d. 06.09.1952)

Matches: 283

Batting:

Runs	HS	Av	100s
9,441	129	24.4	8

Bowling:

Wkts	Av	BB
1	168	1-21

Catches: 211

Two of Lancashire's greatest names were still involved with the club when A.H. took over as captain for seven years. His father was President for the whole period and Archie MacLaren, previously the club's captain for twelve years, was occasionally available to play. Those powerful figures must have had some influence on the young Hornby. He opened with MacLaren in his early years and played the odd game with his father in the side.

Albert Henry, like his father, loved hunting, fishing and riding and inherited many of his father's characteristics. Educated at Harrow and Cambridge, he represented his university, where he made his first-class debut. His first game for Lancashire was against the MCC at Lord's and his Old Trafford debut was against Sussex, opening with Archie MacLaren.

A positive, hard-hitting, dashing opener, his batting was tinged with daring. Opening the innings for most of his career, he was quite content to drop down the order, occasionally to 7 or 8, if the team benefited. A.H. was worth his place in the top six among a strong group of players but his future captaincy was crucial in his maintaining a permanent presence throughout his career. His driving was particularly effective and he was a strong back-foot player. George Beldam photographed him for his famous book to demonstrate the off-drive.

Albert Henry made his mark as a determined and fearless captain, gallant and purposeful in his strong leadership. He learnt to work with the professionals and gain their

respect. Leading from the front, he would take responsibility rather than thrust an unpopular situation on a professional. If a suicidal silly point was required he would stand there. On occasions he would patrol the boundary if an opposition big hitter came in. He caught some spectacular running catches. His problem as captain was an absence of quality bowlers, so the Championship was never achieved in his time, although he led them to second place in 1909.

In his last season he represented the Gentlemen against the Players at Lord's, opening the batting with C.B. Fry. In the second innings he top-scored in the match with 69 against a high bowling attack which included the world's best in S.F. Barnes. A.H. held the Lancashire 7th wicket partnership record of 245 with Jack Sharp and scored a century in forty-three minutes against Somerset at Old Trafford, both remaining records for over eighty years. During his career he scored almost 10,000 first-class runs with a top score of 129 against a strong Surrey side.

A most respected leader of his team, he criticised the Lancashire Committee in a *Manchester Guardian* article for suggesting a reduction of playing staff and fewer games to balance the books. He would not have his players treated shabbily.

After military service in the First World War, he bought an estate of 375 acres to farm in Ireland, sixteen miles from Cork to enjoy once again his hunting and salmon fishing.

Born: Blackburn, 10.02.1847 (d. 17.12.1925)

Matches: 292

Batting:

Runs	HS	Av	100s
10,649	188	24.2	10

Bowling:

Wkts	Av	BB
3	31.3	1-2

Catches: 217

Tests: 3

Albert Nelson Hornby is the most influential person in the long history of Lancashire County Cricket Club. Born in Blackburn in 1847, he was the sixth son of William Henry, a wealthy cotton industrialist, deputy lieutenant of the county of Lancashire and first mayor of Blackburn. He sent his son Albert to Harrow School, where he loved to play cricket. As a junior he was only 4ft 7in tall and weighed 6 stones. Hornby was given the nickname 'Monkey' because of his small stature. At 17 years and stronger, he was opening the innings for Harrow. Going up to Oxford, he was told his cricket would be limited because of academic study. He made a hurried departure to follow his overriding passion, playing as much cricket as he could. Hornby scored several centuries in minor matches, including 141 for Whalley when nineteen years old and 201 for Cheshire against Shropshire. He made his Lancashire debut at twenty years of age at Whalley in a Roses game. Within three years he was their foremost batsman, scoring over 2,000 runs in all forms of cricket, including his maiden first-class century against Hampshire at Southampton.

Gaining respect throughout his country as a right-hand hard-hitting opening batsman, this pugnacious player stepped out of the pavilion in a brisk, positive manner, leaving his batting partner to catch up. Hair parted in the middle and with a short, military moustache, this dapper batsman of medium height but thickly set figure was well known for his aggressive style,

enthusiasm and keen devotion to county cricket. The amateur cricketer was pampered at Old Trafford, having the best conditions in the main pavilion on the north side of the ground. His opening partner Richard Barlow changed in the pros' pavilion on the opposite side of the ground. The two openers met at the wicket for the opening ball. When Hornby became captain he changed this practice and all players changed in the main pavilion, though different dressing rooms.

Early in their opening partnership, Hornby and Barlow set a record unequalled in 1875. In the Roses game at Old Trafford Lancashire commenced their second innings requiring 146 to win on a bowler's pitch against a strong Yorkshire attack. They achieved this total without either losing his wicket. In 1878 Hornby persuaded W.G. Grace and brothers to bring their Gloucestershire side to Old Trafford for the first time. They were the champion county. Hornby made the only century in the match, outplaying the famous Grace brothers. The vivacious Hornby's strategy was to run as soon as the ball was hit. Barlow adjusted to the sprinting, learning quickly to dash or be run out. Their style was entertaining and match-winning. When Hornby joined the club, only 200 spectators came to watch Lancashire but over 28,000 attended the Gloucestershire game including one budding writer and poet, Francis Thompson, who almost thirty years later was to reminisce on the excitement of watching the Lancashire openers. He composed the most famous cricket poem in the world with the haunting lines: 'as the run-stealers flicker to and fro, to and fro, O my Hornby and my Barlow long ago'.

Hornby was appointed captain in 1880 and brought immediate success to the county. They won the Championship outright in 1881, when they were unbeaten, and shared the title in 1982 and 1989. After MacLaren's years as captain, Hornby was asked to come back to lead the side and he inspired them to top the Championship table again in 1897. His leadership brought the best out of his men. Fair and faithful to his professional colleagues, they became loyal to him. He possessed a great sense of humour and sound judgement. On occasions he could be a strict disciplinarian in a military, brisk way; when players did not show his keen attitude, he was most annoyed at any slackness. He could be a stern and unyielding adversary, an attitude which invaded his approach to cricket.

Leading by example, the captain was the county's highest scorer for twelve years. He became the only batsman to score centuries on the poor pitches over that time. The first player to score 1,000 runs in a season for his county, he topped the national averages in his second year as captain, making 1,531 runs averaging over 40. In his career he made 17 first-class hundreds, his highest score being 188 against Derbyshire at Old Trafford. He also scored 161 against a strong Surrey side.

A.N. Hornby's first overseas tour was to North America with MCC secretary Fitzgerald in 1872. He toured with Lord Harris' team to play in his first Test match at Sydney against Australia. On that tour Harris was attacked by a spectator and Hornby, although assaulted himself, marched the offender to the pavilion. He captained England twice against Australia, in 1882 at The Oval in that famous game when the Ashes were born and in the first Test match at Old Trafford in 1884. Playing over 30 games for the Gentlemen *v.* Players, he also captained the MCC on occasions, including their centenary match.

An occasional bowler, left or right-handed depending on his mood, he was also a brilliant fielder anywhere. Fielding at Lord's, the enthusiastic Hornby dashed after a ball towards the boundary, scattering spectators with the result that one elderly man was injured. He pointed out to the authorities that this could happen regularly and at Hornby's suggestion, the boundary line was established in county cricket.

His inherited wealth and marriage to the daughter of the owner of *London Illustrated News* meant he was able to play sport all his active life. In rural Cheshire he was a master horse rider, a respected hunter of hounds and a skilful shooter. In his early years he was a competent boxer and an excellent sprinter and hurdler. Soccer was another of his many sporting activities and he represented Blackburn Rovers on many occasions. He played rugby union for the North versus the South and captained the England rugby union team, playing 9 internationals between 1877 and 1882.

A.N. Hornby was the longest serving President of Lancashire County Cricket Club, holding the position for twenty-three years. Known as the Squire of Lancashire cricket, for decades he was the very soul of the club. He was happiest playing the game. His last first-class match was for an England XI in 1906, aged fifty-nine. He scored 53 runs, I suspect relatively quickly.

Nigel Howard
RHB, 1946-53

Born: Hyde, 18.05.1925 (d. 31.05.1979)

Matches: 170

Batting:

Runs	HS	Av	100s
5,526	145	26.9	3

Catches: 131

Tests: 4

A good captain may have to sacrifice some of his own high ability as a batsman to give his energies towards leading and bringing a united consistency to a group of opinionated individuals. Senior and junior professionals have their own agenda and one of Nigel Howard's strengths was to give young players an early chance. He was pushed to the front early in his career and learnt how an injection of confidence improved performance. It was his leadership qualities as captain of Lancashire, the Gentlemen of England and his country on tour to India that enabled Nigel to make his mark.

As an attractive right-hand batsman with a wide variety of strokes, he had topped the Rossall School's batting averages at the end of the war. The information had filtered through to Lancashire and Nigel joined the staff after his degree at Manchester University. He was regarded as one of the most promising amateurs in 1946. His father Rupert, a former major in the Army, was secretary of the Lancashire Club and had managed the MCC in Australia for two tours, one either side of the war. Barry, his younger brother, was a promising cricketer who later played for the county, so brother Nigel was steeped in cricketing tradition.

In June 1948 he played against Worcestershire, batting at No.7 behind a strong line up of Washbrook, Place, Edrich, Ikin, Cranston and Wharton, and displayed his stylish aggression by scoring 80. Immediately he was moved up the order and made 93 at Liverpool against Northampton. Opening with Winston Place

at Old Trafford that season he scored his maiden century against Derbyshire, 145 in four hours including 14 fours.

Elected captain of the club in 1949 after Ken Cranston retired, he was, at twenty-three years of age, the youngest leader in Lancashire's history after Archie MacLaren. Responsibilities at such a tender age had an effect, but the following year he was back on form and made over 1,100 runs for the county, including a fine unbeaten century against Gloucestershire at Old Trafford. More importantly, his leadership brought the Championship back to Lancashire, shared with Surrey. No doubt he leant on the wise council of Cyril Washbrook for his success.

Captaining the MCC on the winter tour of India in February 1951, he led the side most capably but developed pleurisy in the second half of the tour. Returning to England he recovered to make his highest score at Maidstone the following summer, an unbeaten 138 against Kent. A good driver and particularly severe on the leg side, he hit 24 fours and a six.

Nigel Howard retired from cricket at twenty-eight years of age to concentrate on his family textile business. A fine all-round sportsman, he had represented Cheshire at hockey and golf. In 1976 he retired to the Isle of Man where he died three years later at fifty-four.

Bill Huddleston
RHB & RMOB, 1899-1914

Born: Earlestown, 27.02.1873 (d. 21.05.1962)

Matches: 183

Batting:

Runs	HS	Av
2,765	88	12.2

Bowling:

Wkts	Av	BB
684	17.5	9-36

Catches: 149

A tall man with a high action, Bill Huddleston bowled medium-paced off-breaks. With a fairly easy-going nature, he had a smooth, unlaboured action. Born at Earlestown near Newton-le-Willows, he was an exceptional bowler in league cricket, making his living as professional first for Todmorden and then for Church Cricket Club. His success as opening bowler for Church came to the notice of the Lancashire Committee who invited him to play for the county against the Australians at Liverpool in August 1899. He was allowed only 5 overs, from which the Australians scored only 9 runs and in the following match against Middlesex at Old Trafford he took his first wicket.

All eyes were on the great S.F. Barnes in Lancashire's XI and Bill Huddleston was ignored. The women suffragettes struggling for the right to vote were forcing attention on parliament as Bill was seeking his chance to be noticed by the Lancashire Committee. He had proved he could perform. In a month at The Oval in the Championship season of 1904, Surrey were left with 337 to win and had reached 206 for 2 at lunchtime. Bill was given the ball as second change and the last 8 wickets were dismissed for 60, his off spin taking 7 for 22.

Taking a clutch of wickets on drying pitches yet few on dry turf, Lancashire viewed Huddleston as an enigma. Interestingly he made his debut when Elgar wrote his *Variations on a Theme*. On the verge of regular selection for several seasons, he finally made a place for himself in 1906 when Elgar responded by composing his famous *Pomp and Circumstance No.4* in celebration. That year brought success for them both, the bowler topping the averages with 50 wickets from only 9 matches. He was tied to a contract with Church Cricket Club so was unavailable for part of the season.

The following season was full time and Huddleston took up the challenge, increasing his dismissals. The wet summer helped enormously as he rattled the stumps regularly, taking 71 wickets at only 13 runs each. The best batsmen in the land couldn't master his accurate, spinning deliveries. He clean-bowled C.B. Fry for a duck at Liverpool, Frank Woolley twice for low scores at Old Trafford and the Gunn brothers against Nottinghamshire. 12 wickets were his against Surrey and 12 more against Warwickshire. He had won his vote from the Lancashire Committee who admitted he should have been picked more regularly.

Each season passed with continued success and impressive figures. In fair summers when it was felt he was less effective he played fewer games, as in 1911, but still topped the bowling averages. As the First World War threatened, he reached his best season with 110 Championship wickets taken and 500 runs scored. His 88 against Yorkshire was his best innings and then the war changed direction for everyone. After the war, he played league cricket for many years and coached his valued cricket skills at Harrow school.

David Hughes
RHB & SLA, 1967-91

Born: Newton-Le-Willows, 13.05.1947

Matches: 436

Batting:

Runs	HS	Av	100s
10,126	153	22	8

Bowling:

Wkts	Av	BB
637	29.7	7-24

Catches: 325

In reflecting with admiration the all-round skills of David Paul Hughes, one has to place his astute leadership of the team at the head of these qualities. Appointed captain in 1987 for a five-year spell, he led a floundering and struggling Lancashire side from the bottom end of the Championship table, where they had been for over ten years, to second place, almost winning the competition. The new captain possessed a most positive attitude, encouraging the best out of his colleagues, building confidence and achieving excellent results.

Born in the Lancashire town of Newton-le-Willows, the Manchester Association witnessed the developing left-arm spin bowling of the promising Hughes. He was invited to join Lancashire in 1966 at just nineteen years of age. With a short run-up and easy left-arm action, he used flight and variety of controlled spin with accurate line and length from the beginning. David's best years as a bowler were under Jack Bond's captaincy, taking almost 300 wickets in the first five years.

Used regularly in the successful one-day competition in tandem with his pal Jack Simmons, he produced the Sunday League competition best with 6-29 against Somerset. A vital ingredient in limited-overs bowling was economy, and with a flatter delivery he was quicker and more difficult to hit. That variety was extended to Championship matches. 243 wickets in limited-overs matches at a miserly average of 23 proved his consistent accuracy and he became a vital ingredient in the trophy-winning sides with both bat and ball.

Batting blossomed when bowling declined and after scoring 1,000 runs in 1981, he repeated the feat the following year with an average of almost 50. An aggressive right-handed batsman, he could clear the field hitting cleanly, as demonstrated in the famous one-day Gillette Cup game against Gloucestershire in the late evening. He hit 24 in 1 exciting over to turn the match. There were graceful cover drives as well as pulls on the leg side in his artillery and a technically sound defence. 'Yozzer' was also a brilliant fielder throughout his long career, particularly in the covers. Finally he accepted the manager's position to complete his all-round contribution.

He would wish to be remembered mainly as a bowler but it is his all-round natural ability in every department that makes him different. In each phase of his development he made a major contribution to his county. He is intelligent and possesses a dry sense of humour. His alert presence has steered him into a successful career in sports hospitality.

Born: Mawdesley, 08.01.1902 (d. 17.04.1946)

Matches: 483

Batting:

Runs	HS	Av	100s
21,975	222	37	46

Bowling:

Wkts	Av	BB
533	26.6	9-42

Catches: 207

Tests: 5

He looked immaculate on the field. The impeccably creased white flannels and dapper trim neatness emphasised the naturally athletic batsman's classical style expressing a wide range of stylish strokes. With a wristy action and natural body movement, he was able to manipulate all types of bowling through the field.

Although one of Lancashire's most successful all-rounders, he was too good a batsman to practice the concentration required of a great bowler. One of only four Lancastrians to have scored 10,000 runs and taken 500 wickets, he made over 22,000 first-class runs which included a hundred against every other county.

Jack Iddon came from a cricketing family, his father being professional to Lancaster Cricket Club for fourteen years. Jack's league clubs were Adlington and Leyland Motors before he played for his county against Oxford University at twenty-two years. He soon made his mark as an all-rounder, playing a major part in the 5 Championship wins. His most prolific season was the Championship year of 1934 when he scored 2,261 runs averaging over 55. Five double centuries were included in his 46 centuries and he was also involved in record-breaking batting partnerships for Lancashire.

Bowling slow left-arm spinners, he was most dangerous on wearing wickets. At Sheffield in 1937 he accomplished his best analysis of 9 for 42 to help beat Yorkshire by 5 wickets. In the wet season of 1932 he headed the bowling averages with 76 wickets at 16 runs each. His fielding was exceptional anywhere, returning the ball over the stumps to George Duckworth with a quick response and flick of the wrist.

Jack played in 5 Test matches, 4 against the West Indies in 1934/35 where he scored 73 at Port of Spain and another half century at Kingston. The fifth was against South Africa at Trent Bridge the following summer. His only other tour was to Jamaica with Sir Julien Cahn in 1928/29.

Like many other good players, the war interrupted his career. Turning amateur for the few games in 1945, he was one of a handful of cricketers being considered as captain when full-time county cricket resumed.

In the winter he was a technical representative to a firm of brake-lining experts in Manchester and was returning home from a business visit to the Rolls Royce works in Crewe when he was killed in a motor accident a month before the season started. He left a wife and two children who were awarded with damages of £9,801.

Jack Iddon was good at most sports, playing soccer for Bolton Wanderers. At cricket he was a gifted all-rounder who contributed much to the winning of 5 Championships.

Born: Bignall End, 07.03.1918 (d. 15.09.1984)

Matches: 288

Batting:

Runs	HS	Av	100s
14,327	192	37.7	23

Bowling:

Wkts	Av	BB
278	28.7	6-21

Catches: 329

Tests: 18

A courteous, dark, good-looking cricketer, neatly proportioned at average height, Jack Ikin made his first appearance for Lancashire against the West Indies tourists in 1939. For this gifted cricketer the war came too soon, with service in the eighth army as a Desert Rat in Tobruck.

Returning to Old Trafford after demob, Jack was given a Test trial at Lord's and was picked for the first 2 Tests against India. In between those matches he scored his maiden century for Lancashire against the tourists and earned his county cap after his England award.

It was his all-round ability that attracted Test selectors. A graceful left-handed batsman with a strong top hand, he played stylish strokes all round the wicket. He faced fast bowlers with courage and determination and was comfortable opening or in the middle order, an adaptable and reliable batsman.

Jack bowled accurate leg-breaks and googlies with the occasional deceptive top-spinner. A strong group of spinners at Lancashire gave him less opportunity than he deserved. He was a brilliant, alert, close-to-the-wicket fielder, usually at short leg. With his watchful, relaxed pose, it seemed he was as quick as light catching a ball the eye could not glimpse. The close-to-the-wicket trio of Ken Grieves, Geoff Edrich and Jack Ikin poached catches with uncommon anticipation; nothing seemed to pass that reliable barrier. Between them they caught over 1,200 victims in Lancashire matches.

Chosen for tours to Australia and the West Indies, he played in 18 Test matches. He never settled as comfortably in an England shirt as he did over twelve memorable seasons with Lancashire where he made his great all-round contribution. He reached 1,000 runs ten times. Early in his career he twice carried his bat through a completed innings and made his highest score of 192 against Oxford University. His best bowling statistics appeared early in his career with 6 for 21 against Nottinghamshire in 1947. He took a hat-trick at Taunton two years later.

Recurring ill health from the mid-1950s affected his career. He was a most respected and loved cricketer. The public gave him a successful benefit against Surrey in 1953 and a Manchester accountant who greatly admired the all-rounder left him a small fortune – such was his popularity. Jack devoted his time to schools cricket and on retirement from the county scene became a coach at Denstone College. He captained Staffordshire and the Minor Counties, was elected honorary member of the MCC and a Vice-President of Lancashire County Cricket Club.

Peter Lee
RHB & RMF, 1972-82

Born: Arthingworth, 27.08.1945

Matches: 152

Batting:

Runs	HS	Av
500	25	7.6

Bowling:

Wkts	Av	BB
496	23.8	8-34

Catches: 18

Taking part in Northamptonshire's pre-season training in 1972, Peter received an offer from Lancashire, who were searching for a fast bowler to support Lever and Shuttleworth, both of whom were possible Test selections. Opportunities seemed brighter at Lancashire and he made his debut at Old Trafford against the Australians in early May, taking 5 wickets in the match. Making an immediate impact in all forms of cricket, including a 4 for 17 display against Derbyshire in the Sunday League, Peter also played an important part in winning the Gillette Cup final at Lord's in his first season. He was capped on the same day as Frank Hayes.

In only his second season with Lancashire he was one of only two county bowlers – and the only Englishman – to achieve 100 first-class wickets. 'Leapy' Lee was the first Lancashire bowler to do so since Ken Higgs five years earlier. His consistent line and length with the ability to swing the ball each way outwitted top players as well as tail-enders. Early in his Lancashire career, he was one of the fittest bowlers, ever present in the side, bowling marathon spells without complaint. Pete was always grateful to Jack Mercer, the influential coach in his youth who had suggested Brian Statham as an ideal model, and to play for the same county was a bonus.

Two seasons later he took 112 first-class wickets averaging 18 each, once again the only

Englishman to do so. It was a special achievement in a summer of glorious weather and good batting conditions. Wisden recognised his ability by making him one of their five cricketers of the year in 1975. Leapy played his part again in a most successful season, winning the Gillette Cup final at Lord's. The best Lancashire bowler for the next two seasons was rewarded by his fourth visit to a final at Lord's.

Invited to join private tours to South Africa twice with D.H. Robins and to the West Indies with an English Counties XI gave him valuable experience but little rest. In the season of 1978 he suffered a serious shoulder injury which led to an operation. It affected his future performances, although two years later he achieved his best figures of 8 for 34 against Oxford University. His last first-class wicket was Geoffrey Boycott in a Roses match in 1982 and he retired to the North East Leagues to be the professional at Gateshead Fell as well as playing minor counties cricket for Durham. He soon moved to Dudley to be professional in the Birmingham League.

Leapy missed out on a benefit at Lancashire which he richly deserved. He works in the building trade near Northampton where he lives with his wife Jane and two daughters. Still enjoying the game, he plays for his Earls Barton local league. He always gave of his best, a humble, amiable chap, a great professional and a model team member. He joins us regularly at Old Trafford as a member of the Lancashire Players' Association.

Born: Todmorden, 17.09.1940

Matches: 268

Batting:

Runs	HS	Av
3,073	83	13.5

Bowling:

Wkts	Av	BB
716	24.6	7-70

Catches: 89

Tests: 17

A long, workmanlike run with arms pumping away characterised the fair-haired Peter Lever. He could increase his speed of delivery on occasions and bowl a perfect bouncer. At his best he delivered a dangerous away swing from the right-handed bat. A thinking bowler who always gave 100 per cent, he could vary pace and swing. Never a passenger, his strength and extra effort could deliver a surprisingly fast ball. Having that special hunger and a determination to win games, Peter was always a trier who had little time for the languorous and lethargic cricketer.

A Todmorden lad born and bred, he played his first match for Lancashire when he was nineteen years of age. There was keen competition to partner Statham with Higgs, Colin Hilton, Roy Collins and Marner all available. Lever improved each season and came good in 1963 with his first 50 Championship wickets, having had the opportunity to open.

In the mid-1960s he was a capable batsman, picking up 500 runs in a season as well as 60 wickets. In Statham's last season he took 5-39 against Middlesex at Lord's and 6-49 at the same venue the following year as well as a hat-trick against Northamptonshire.

The multi-talented Rest of the World side toured England instead of the South Africans in 1970. The England team was struggling in early matches and Peter Lever's impressive county performances won him a place in the England side at The Oval. His England debut was sensational, 7 wickets for 83 runs with top-class batsmen Eddie Barlow, Graeme Pollock, Gary Sobers, Mushtaq, Clive Lloyd and Mike Proctor among his victims. Few bowlers in the post-war period have accomplished such devastation in 33 overs. This magnificent day drew the attention of selectors, and he was picked to go to Australia the following winter. There, on a placid Adelaide wicket, he took 4 for 49 and, often chosen to bowl into the wind, he played his part in regaining the Ashes and contributed to the excellent team spirit on tours.

Batting for England encouraged his best scores; 88 not out against India at Old Trafford and 3 century stands against New Zealand and Pakistan in his 17 Test matches.

He retained an immense passion for the game on retirement and was invited to coach the national team as well as giving time from his successful business to coach the Lancashire bowlers.

Born: Freshfield, 11.10.1911 (d. 29.07.1998)

Matches: 158

Batting:

Runs	HS	Av	100s
3,561	104*	18.4	2

Bowling:

Wkts	Av	BB
1	74	1-10

Catches: 69

Amateur captains of average ability seldom held the respect of professional players over a lengthy period but Lionel Lister was always referred to as 'Skipper' by his team well after his retirement. This loyalty was deserved by a leader who was a perfect gentleman, treating all his players with great respect and getting the best from them. In conversation with him in his seventies he still praised the members of his team; no hint of a negative remark was uttered.

Son of the Cunard Shipping Company's managing director, he attended Malvern School and Cambridge. He studied law, though he was wealthy enough to enjoy most of his life playing sport. A gifted all-rounder, he played in 4 amateur soccer internationals at wing-half and turned down the chance to sign professional forms with Liverpool and Blackpool Football Clubs. Lister was a fine golfer and played club cricket with Formby near Southport.

In 1933 he was invited to play for Lancashire as an amateur and scored an undefeated century in his second game against Middlesex at Old Trafford. His partnership with Frank Sibbles produced 165 runs in one and three-quarter hours with attractive off-drives and shots all round the wicket. The following year he acted as deputy captain on many occasions when Peter Eckersley was absent and helped to bring the Championship to Lancashire. He recalled with pleasure batting with Eddie Paynter at Alexandra Meadows, Blackburn, racing to a 140 partnership in one and a half hours and an almost identical partnership with Ernest Tyldesley at Old Trafford for another critical win.

In 1936 he was elected captain. At Lord's that year he hit the only century of the match. Neville Cardus talked of Lister's magnificent drives and delicate late cuts as he raced to his undefeated century in only one and a half hours.

Three years later he was padded up to bat at Northampton when a call came through to report to the Royal Artillery immediately. The captain said farewell to his team mates not realising it would be his last first-class match. As brigade major he continued to lead a company of men in the Normandy landings.

Lionel Lister was the first to acknowledge his own limitations as a first-class cricketer. It was his irresistible, persuasive charm, his intelligence and acquired wisdom, his unbridled popularity and respect from his players that made him special.

Clive Lloyd

LHB & RM, 1968-86

Born: Georgetown, 31.08.1944

Matches: 219

Batting:

Runs	HS	Av	100s
12,764	217*	44.9	30

Bowling:

Wkts	Av	BB
55	32.8	4-48

Catches: 161

Tests: 110

A towering figure in the world of cricket, Clive was one of the greatest overseas cricketers to play in county cricket and fortunately he chose the friendly people of Lancashire to entertain for almost twenty years. Born in Georgetown, his father died when he was fourteen years old and, as the oldest of six children, it was his responsibility to support the family so plans for further education were interrupted. Joining Haslingden as professional in the Lancashire League, he was approached by Lancashire County Cricket Club to join the staff.

His massive presence and influence was immediate and in 1969 Clive contributed to Lancashire's success in winning the John Player-sponsored National League title in its inaugural year. Soon he was topping the Lancashire batting averages, a record he managed in 11 seasons. Trophies came along regularly, Lancashire retaining the National League title in 1970 as well as winning the first of three consecutive major cup competitions sponsored by Gillette. Clive averaged over 50 in those one-day competitions and his tight bowling and brilliant fielding played a major part in the team's continued success. His explosive batting hit the headlines and thousands of spectators came to watch, many locked outside the ground on occasions. In the Championship he hit a quick double century against Warwickshire and finished the 1970 season as the fastest run-maker in the Championship.

The third Gillette Cup final at Lord's was won by an inspired century from 'Big Hubert'.

He exhibited tremendous power, the ball hitting the boundary before fielders could move, such was his awesome hitting. Lancashire were not the same team when he toured England with the West Indies in 1973, when he made more runs than any other player for his country in Tests and tour games. The following year he was appointed captain of his national side and during his next tour he scored another record unbeaten 242 against India at Bombay.

The first World Cup was held in England in 1975 and Clive's West Indies team claimed the trophy. The whole of Lord's was alive with West Indian rhythms as the tall majestic Lloyd, brimming with a mixture of power, elegance and grace, hit cleanly from the front and back foot against a strong Australian attack. The ferocity of hitting was unforgettable. The knowledgeable Denis Compton, along with many others, called it the greatest innings they had seen and compared it with the 1938 innings of Stan McCabe when Bradman beckoned all his players to the balcony, making the comment that they may never see the like again. But they had, suggested Compton, all of thirty-seven years later.

Clive Lloyd had huge strength, using bats one and a half times heavier than most players. His large hands clasped the thick, long handle covered in three rubber sleeves. The combination of enormous strength, great reach, natural timing and his instinctive attacking urge made him one of the most destructive and effectively powerful controlled hitters in the history of cricket. He could turn a match in an hour and often did in all forms of cricket. Wearing a floppy sun hat in the heat of the summer's day, this bespectacled giant ambled nonchalantly to the wicket like an amiable Paddington Bear. Surveying the field, he unleashed a variety of powerful drives and shots from the back foot all round the wicket with formidable authority.

The following season he equalled the fastest double century in first-class cricket when the West Indies played Glamorgan at Swansea. His 200 came in 122 balls. Gilbert Jessop's seventy-three-year-old record was timed in two hours. Clive equalled that time, which included a three-minute stoppage for drinks.

The presence of Clive Lloyd in the covers was enough to cause uncertainty among any opposing batsmen. He was like a great cat pouncing on the ball and in one action, with a whip of a mighty arm, propelling it flat to break the stumps. Lancashire supporters relished the first sight of this action in their first Gillette Cup win against Sussex when he moved like lightning in the covers to run out 3 batsmen.

There was no greater team player than Clive Lloyd. He never placed personal records or averages above the needs of his side. His unselfish devotion to Lancashire was demonstrated when he was in great pain requiring a cartilage operation. A Gillette Cup match was imminent against Surrey at Old Trafford. He could hardly walk to the wicket and quick singles were out of the question. Carrying this handicap he smashed 86 runs from 71 balls including 6 sixes.

Clive was the West Indies' longest-serving and most distinguished captain. Under his leadership he produced the strongest Test side in the world for almost ten years. His great strength was man management, uniting a group of happy-go-lucky calypso players into an organised, professional team. He blended different personalities from different islands into one cohesive unit. There was criticism of his use of a constant battery of aggressive fast bowlers, seldom employing a spinner. His answer was to study the results. A great disciplinarian on and off the field, he fought for better conditions for his players and led by example, always remaining approachable and making calm decisions against an often hostile political background. He led his side in 74 Test matches, beaten only in 2 series out of the 18 he captained and played 27 Tests without a defeat. His batting average as captain was more than 50 runs for each innings.

Clive Lloyd was a colossus in West Indian and Lancashire cricket. The home crowd stirred in anticipation and bars were emptied when the gentle giant walked down the steps onto the field. There was a slightly forward stoop as he walked to the wicket, unconcerned, bat under his arm. He was a quiet but strong influential force in his time at Lancashire where he captained the side for four years. In later years he had unconsciously become a national ambassador, an unflappable, dignified elder statesman. He continued to serve Lancashire cricket after playing, appointed Vice-President and joining the Committee for many years.

He gave us many magic moments on summer days. The lasting memory is the sight and sound of a tall, distinguished, left-handed adopted Lancastrian swinging a huge bat, dispatching the ball to the furthest corners of every cricket ground. Those who saw him witnessed a special moment in Lancashire's history.

David Lloyd
LHB & SLA, 1965-83

Born: 18.03.1947

Matches: 378

Batting:

Runs	HS	Av	100s
17,877	195	33.4	37

Bowling:

Wkts	Av	BB
234	29.9	7-38

Catches: 311

Tests: 9

Born in the heart of the Lancashire leagues, the young David Lloyd played ball games in the Lowry-like back streets of Accrington. It was a friendly, caring community where a quick wit, plain speaking and honest humour were helpful survival qualities. David learnt his cricket in the demanding nursery of the Lancashire leagues, a competitive environment with Methodist values. He was soon playing representation games for Lancashire Schoolboys and on leaving school he joined Lancashire County Cricket Club.

As a slow bowler and middle-order batsman of promise, Bumble was a thoughtful, positive cricketer. His nickname, 'Bumble', came from the eccentric comedian Michael Bentine's bumble men. In his second year he took 7 for 38 against Gloucestershire at Lydney, his best analysis. When Jack Bond became captain in 1968, Bumble was promoted to open the innings and made his maiden century, an unbeaten 148 against Cambridge University at Fenners, putting on 194 in three hours with Harry Pilling. He made the first of his 1,000 runs a season, achieving this mark ten times. Bumble was good humoured and talkative. Full of nervous energy and with a lively mind, he was a good team man, especially in the dressing room and on tour.

In one-day games Farokh Engineer was his opening partner. In the longer game Barry Wood shared three opening partnerships of over 250 with him. Success came when the Sunday League was born. The team won the

League twice plus a trio of Gillette Cup wins in the early 1970s. He scored a century in all three major one-day competitions and in 1972 scored 6 centuries in county cricket, averaging 47 that year.

When Jack Bond retired, Bumble's fine displays and cricket brain earned him the captaincy for the next five years, leading his team to the Gillette Cup final three seasons in succession and winning the trophy in 1975.

Invited to play for England in 1974, Bumble scored an unbeaten 214 against India at Edgbaston and was invited to Australia the following winter. In his first-class career he scored over 19,000 runs with a bonus of 237 wickets. In addition there were 7,000 runs and 200 wickets in one-day games.

Retiring from the first-class game he returned to his Accrington club as well as representing Cumberland for five years. There was a year of first-class umpiring, marketing Kwik Cricket for juniors, a spell as an innovative coach for Lancashire and then coaching for the England team. He was in great demand as an after-dinner speaker because of his unique humour, embroidering tales about ordinary characters in the game. Bumble seemed to make his presence felt, enjoyed success and always entertained in whatever role he chose.

Born: Accrington, 01.07.1969

Matches: 200

Batting:

Runs	HS	Av	100s
11,038	241	38	24

Bowling:

Wkts	Av	BB
2	220	1-4

Catches: 140

Graham was playing alongside his father at Accrington CC when a youth training scheme place at sixteen years took him to Lancashire.

No one disliked Graham. An easy going, pleasant character with a dry sense of humour, he was popular in the dressing room as well as with members. He had natural talent, good at football and tennis but particularly blessed with a batsman's gift of quick hand-eye coordination. He was a natural run-scorer and played to entertain. A mischievous risk-taker, he regularly employed the reverse sweep to confuse bowlers. To be fair, he was probably the best performer of this frustrating, unorthodox shot but on occasions it has caused his downfall. It was never a boring session watching Graham bat. A magnificent fielder anywhere, he was gifted with natural speed and strength. There seemed a sudden transformation from his casual, rustic farmer's walk to a rapid sprint and a whipped flat throw to wicketkeeper. He was equally effective as a slip fielder.

Making his maiden century against Oxford University at nineteen years, he went on to score 24 centuries plus 3 in the one-day National League. In 1996 his remarkable double century at Chelmsford was reached in 141 balls. He finished with 241, including 12 sixes and 25 fours, a record 4th wicket stand with Titchard of 358 and one that is likely to stand for many years. He recorded the highest score at Headingley in a Roses game and the highest against Yorkshire by any player when he launched a furious attack to plunder 225 from only 151 balls on a slow, low pitch which made timing difficult. Another rapid unbeaten double century came against Derbyshire at Old Trafford.

His international honours included an England 'A' tour of Australia with a century in New South Wales. He played for the full England side in six one-day matches against Australia, Pakistan and South Africa.

Graham won the Walter Lawrence Trophy for the fastest century of the season two years running including the match at Chelmsford and a century in 73 balls at Leicester the following year. He played a major part in the double cup wins of 1996 and 1998 and the NatWest Cup-winning side of 1999. His final century was scored before lunch (rarely achieved in modern county cricket) against Somerset at Old Trafford in 2000.

Having scored over 11,000 first-class runs plus over 5,000 in limited-overs, he retired at the end of the 2002 season, receiving a standing ovation from the crowd in his last game. It was richly deserved for a respected, considerate cricketer who felt it a duty to entertain.

Ted McDonald

RHB & RF, 1924-31

Born: Launceston, 06.01.1891 (d. 22.07.1937)

Matches: 217

Batting:

Runs	HS	Av	100s
1,868	100*	10.1	1

Bowling:

Wkts	Av	BB
1,053	20.9	8-53

Catches: 78

Tests: 11

No other Lancashire cricketer made a greater contribution to the triple Championship successes in the mid-1920s. Edgar Arthur McDonald played only six full seasons and two half summers with Lancashire but his presence in that short time was that of a colossus, lifting and motivating the side to major honours. Surprisingly, he was thirty-three when he arrived for his first part season.

Born in Tasmania, McDonald made his Test debut at the mature age of thirty years. Chosen to tour England the following summer, McDonald and his opening partner Gregory proved to be a ravaging, destructive bowling force. He captured more Test wickets than any other bowler on either side and took 150 wickets at an average of 15.9. After the 1921 tour he joined Nelson CC and three years later signed a contract with Lancashire on a residential qualification.

McDonald's 16-yard run-up revealed a beautiful, rhythmical action, smooth and graceful. He approached the wicket in a slightly curving track, silently gliding over the grass. He left no rough footmarks, even at the end of the day. Seemingly with little effort, his curved wrist delivered a ball as pacey as any bowler of his day, making the ball lift dangerously even from a good length. There was late outswing with the new ball and when it became worn, he could break it back into the right-handed batsman. They nicknamed him the 'Quiet Destroyer'.

Tall but not heavily built, with a lithe, agile frame strongly sinewed, his casual, detached nature disguised a slight flaw. He was a man of few words and could be moody, phlegmatic on occasions. There were times when he bowled a series of bouncers which unnerved the best of batsmen. Players wore little protection in the 1920s and his bowling was thought to be provocative on these occasions. Sometimes McDonald was unpredictable, experimenting with slow off-spinners when the mood suited him. In one match against Kent he was bowling his slow spinners and the whole team had to persuade him to bowl fast when the opponents needed only 65 to win. Len Green ordered a large whisky for Ted at the lunch break. It did the trick and within the next 30 runs McDonald had bowled the side out, getting a hat-trick. He took 12 wickets in the match. That season Lancashire won the Championship and McDonald took 175 wickets for the county.

In 1926, the first of the Championship winning years, it was McDonald more than any other player in the XI who won the matches. His temperament seemed to thrive on a fight where there was a sporting chance to win. Keen to bowl Yorkshire out in the Roses game at Old Trafford, McDonald struck the reliable No.3 batsman Oldroyd on the head with a lifting delivery and, after hospitalisation, he did not play again that season. McDonald finished

E. A.
Macdonald

with 175 wickets and a maiden century at Old Trafford against Middlesex in 100 minutes with fierce hitting.

Another 150 wickets by McDonald the next season helped Lancashire to another Championship title. The appalling weather did not help the bowler in the latter half of the season but he showed his quality by helping to win 8 of the first 11 games. Lancashire lost only once in the summer. A typical early game was the Roses Whitsun Bank Holiday fixture at Old Trafford. Packed with spectators, McDonald bowled at a fine pace, making the ball lift and finishing with 11 wickets for 135 runs giving his side an excellent victory. The next game against Sussex was comparatively poorly attended and McDonald's analysis was 0 for 108 against a weakened side. The following match against Surrey he took 6 wickets in the first innings.

The season of 1928 was Lancashire's third successive Championship win, the side going unbeaten all season. The greatest match-winning factor was again the devastating bowling of McDonald, who captured 190 first-class wickets at 19 runs each. Bowling over 1,250 overs, his form remained outstanding, no other Lancashire bowler taking half his total. He took 15 wickets in an astonishing performance against Kent at Old Trafford. The visitors were 262 for 4 but the last 6 wickets went for 15 runs and they lost by an innings, McDonald taking 8 for 53 in their second innings.

This heavy burden placed on the shoulders of McDonald continued in 1929, when he took 140 Championship wickets supported strongly by Dick Tyldesley. Ted McDonald was granted a benefit match in recognition of his great achievements. He chose Middlesex, took most of the wickets but was unlucky with the August weather. A healthy sum of almost £2,000 assured him that he had chosen the right county.

Finishing runners-up in the Championship that year, Lancashire reclaimed the title in 1930, unbeaten once again. McDonald's pace had lost its fire and he relied on quick off-breaks and variety, although he secured his 100 wickets once more. He earned a third hat-trick at Edgbaston and clean-bowled the great Bradman for 9 at Liverpool.

The summer sun was setting on the magnificent career of this remarkable cricketer. At forty years of age he managed only 14 matches in his final season. By mutual agreement he retired to play league cricket for Bacup where the financial rewards were very satisfactory for less strain on his tiring frame.

He died five years later in a tragic accident. His own car had swerved to avoid collision and turned over. McDonald, unhurt, was fatally knocked down by a passing motorist as he was offering help to the victims of the accident. One wonders if the driver was aware of the great light he had extinguished. Even in another century he is mentioned still when cricket-lovers choose an all-time Lancashire side. Such was his overwhelming contribution and impact on county cricket.

Born: Eastwood, 24.05.1844 (d. 13.09.1892)

Matches: 72

Batting:

Runs	HS	Av
758	66	8.2

Bowling:

Wkts	Av	BB
441	11.6	8-31

Catches: 53

For a few years Bill McIntyre was one of the best bowlers in England. He made an immediate impact when he joined Lancashire at twenty-eight years of age, taking 8 wickets in his first match, 10 in his second, 11 wickets in his third game and 12 in his fourth. In 1872 these were the only first-class matches played by the county, beating Yorkshire and Derbyshire twice each. Bill's wickets in his first years cost him an incredible 5.6 runs each. The dashing Hornby must have been overjoyed that a quality bowler had joined the team.

Bill McIntyre was born in Eastwood in 1844. He played for Northamptonshire (pre-first-class) and Nottinghamshire, who had a strong opening bowling attack with Wootten, J.C. and Alfred Shaw. There were other fast bowlers trying to make their name with the county, including Martin McIntyre, Bill's younger brother. The county had proven strength in bowling and Bill found limited opportunities to show his talent. He played only 14 games for Nottinghamshire and moved up to Lancashire in 1870 to play for Bolton in the leagues. He therefore qualified to play for the county palatine by residence.

Bill was a fast round-arm bowler, the most common type of delivery around that time, the arm not directly above the shoulder but at a lower projectory. It was illegal to bowl above shoulder height before 1864, when overarm as we know it came to be accepted. He was fast and very accurate, although only 5ft 9ins tall

and weighing 12 stones 7lbs. For seven seasons he was Lancashire's outstanding bowler, topping the averages in each of those seasons. He opened the bowling with Sandy Watson and Mr Appleby, who was the best amateur bowler in England. The best testimony of their great efficiency is the comparatively low scores made against them. Lancashire shared the Championship with Nottinghamshire in 1879 with Bill once again heading the bowling averages. He finished his Lancashire career with 441 first-class wickets at an astonishing 11.6 each.

An above average batsman, Bill generally fielded competently at slip. When he was thirty-three years old, the influential A.N. Hornby arranged a match at Bolton against sixteen of his league side for his testimonial. After retiring he was granted an official benefit against W.G. Grace's Gloucestershire at Old Trafford in 1881. The game was well attended although foreshortened when Lancashire won by an innings. Subscriptions to McIntyre from the club were made up to £1,000, a hefty sum in that year. It was an important investment for his family, because Bill died at Prestwich Asylum, north Manchester, in 1892 when he was forty-eight years old, leaving a widow and five children.

Born: Whalley Range, 01.12.1871
(d. 17.11.1944)

Matches: 307

Batting:

Runs	HS	Av	100s
15,772	424	33.3	30

Bowling:

Wkts	Av	BB
1	247	1-44

Catches: 349

Tests: 35

For more than thirty years MacLaren dominated cricket through the Golden Age of the game. He captained England against Australia more times than any cricketer before or since. Many believe he was the greatest captain ever, others believe he showed too many imperfections. Everyone acknowledged his great presence on and off the field. He showed all the necessary leadership qualities but Archie had a most complex character. He was a natural leader, well respected and admired for his tactical awareness of the game and undisputed talent as a batsman. He was at times a warm, amusing, witty raconteur, charming and generous and showing boundless energy, drive and determination with a most positive, optimistic attitude. On other occasions he was tactless, inflexible, unreliable, appearing arrogant and dismissive, certainly no sufferer of those he perceived as fools. Many of his frustrations came from his lack of finances to support the lifestyle most of his close friends enjoyed. They had wealthy inheritances.

MacLaren was born in Whalley Range, in the then fashionable suburbs of Manchester. His father sent him to Harrow School where he captained the cricket XI. Leaving at eighteen years, he was immediately invited to play for a strong Lancashire side at Hove. Two wickets fell early and the Sussex team witnessed the arrival of the confident, aristocratic-looking eighteen-year-old Harrow captain. In just over two hours he powerfully stroked the ball to all parts of the ground, giving no chances in scoring a brilliant century on his debut.

In 1894 he was invited to captain Lancashire at twenty-two years old and his leadership united a disorganised side to make them runners-up in the Championship. Selected to tour Australia in the winter, he made his first appearance for his country at Melbourne against Victoria and hit a magnificent double century; he was the first to do so in Australia in one day. He also made a century in the Final Test at Melbourne.

His amateur status meant he had to earn a living outside cricket, and financial necessity made Archie take a teaching job in Harrow, which meant he missed all Lancashire's matches until breaking up in July. In the summer of 1895 he met up with his father for his first game at Taunton. It was Somerset's first season in the Championship. MacLaren went in first and was seventh out having batted seven hours and fifty minutes for an astonishing 424 runs, surpassing W.G. Grace's record individual score of 344 and setting up an individual batting record that would last for ninety-nine years. A century in each of the last three games, all on different types of wickets, enabled him to top the national averages above W.G.

His absence from the side in the first half of a season meant A.N. Hornby captaining the side for two years but it didn't change the brilliant batting of MacLaren: he hit a magnificent 152 in 3 hours at Bradford in a Roses match and his late charge helped to win the Championship in 1897. In the winter, he went out with England to Australia, captaining the side due to Stoddart's unavailability, and scored a century in his first Test as captain at his favourite Sydney ground. He topped the English Test averages with over 54 and scored over 1,000 runs on tour. At the end of the series he married Maud Power whose father was a wealthy racing owner. Back in England they set up home in an old country mansion in Wokingham.

In 1900 Archie's financial position improved when Lancashire appointed him assistant secretary of the club. He gave up his teaching job, instead writing for newspapers. A full season with his county allowed Archie to head the averages with 5 centuries.

The following winter, as captain of England, he showed his perceptive judgement by choosing the unknown S.F. Barnes, who took 5 for 65 in his first Test innings and topped the bowling averages. MacLaren was the first batsman to score 4 centuries in Test cricket and headed the averages scoring 3 centuries at Sydney where he was prolific.

Over the next years he continued to score heavily, almost 2,000 runs in 1903 including a record opening partnership at Liverpool of 368 with Spooner. The following summer he took Lancashire to the Championship title undefeated.

When MacLaren came in to bat his bearing and mannerisms were those of an aristocrat. All his gestures gave the impression of grandeur. Cardus, who saw him most, called him 'the noblest Roman of them all'. He scored quickly, and Cardus wrote of his magnificence: driving elegantly, hooking and pulling the fastest of bowlers, he 'dismissed the ball from his presence'. He had speed of foot for a big man and played strongly with time to spare from his back foot. In his armoury was a Cardus favourite, that imperious cover drive, powerful and elegant in execution. He had a high backlift with full swing of the bat but he could be obdurate too with a solid, classical defence when necessary. Excellent in the field, fast and reliable whether in the outfield or at slip, he was regarded as one of the best of his day.

MacLaren was an inspirational captain, a master of field placing and years ahead of his time on tactical awareness, where it was acknowledged by his peers he had no superior. The famous C.B. Fry remarked when playing Lancashire that you could feel at once you were playing against a brain. He could sense immediately the weakness in opposition and was a better judge of cricketer than his contemporaries, some of whom were selectors.

War came and Captain MacLaren served in the Royal Army Service Corps. When cricket was resumed in England Archie was in his late forties. In 1921 the all-powerful Australians were unbeaten in all their matches and were on a financial bonus to finish the season all-conquering. MacLaren announced that he could pick a side that would defeat them. He selected no cricketer who had played in the tests that summer and his side beat the mighty Australians at Eastbourne, his shrewd leadership outwitting the tourists. They lost their winning bonus.

Archie was appointed Lancashire's coach to help develop the youth at Old Trafford and as usual requested his salary in advance. In the winter of 1922/23 the MCC sent out a side to Australia and New Zealand to give experience to England's most promising cricketers under the leadership of MacLaren. It included Percy Chapman, Tich Freeman, Harry Tyldesley, Clem Gibson and Geoffrey Wilson, Yorkshire's captain. The Australian public applauded Archie to the wicket on every appearance such was their high regard for him. MacLaren's final match was against the full New Zealand team. He took 5 catches at slip and batted with his old skill, placing the ball between the fielders and scoring an incredible unbeaten 200, his last first-class innings. Archie was fifty-one years of age!

To support his sporting lifestyle, MacLaren had been a banker, schoolmaster, salesman, hotel manager and film extra in Hollywood along with dozens of other jobs. He went tiger shooting in India with Prince Ranjitsinhji and had all the princely qualities of a wealthy gentleman without the financial backing. Eventually the inheritance arrived from Maud's family and they bought a mansion house and several cottages on a 150-acre estate in Berkshire. He lived there until he died aged seventy-two, and his devoted Maud followed him soon afterwards.

MacLaren made a massive impact on English cricket, never to be forgotten. Still his name is on the tongue of Australian and English cricket followers who have any knowledge of cricket's Golden Age.

Harry Makepeace
RHB & LB, 1906-30

Born: Middlesborough, 22.08.1881
(d. 19.12.1952)

Matches: 487

Batting:

Runs	HS	Av	100s
25,207	203	36.3	42

Bowling:

Wkts	Av	BB
42	46.9	4-33

Catches: 194

Tests: 4

Few men have played cricket and football for England. Joseph William Henry Makepeace played 4 Test matches against Australia and 4 football internationals for England, 3 against Scotland and 1 against Wales. He also appeared in 2 FA Cup finals at wing-half for Everton, collecting a winner's medal at Crystal Palace in 1906.

A patient, right-handed batsman, Makepeace developed a solid and stubborn defence. A coaching book technique and the ability to see the ball quickly made him difficult to dislodge. A watchful, courteous player with remarkable powers of concentration, he judged bowlers' length and direction well. He would assist the ball rather than power it to the boundary. There was always quick footwork and good timing. On a bad pitch he had few superiors in cricket.

The First World War interrupted a blossoming career but Harry's batting excelled in the 1920s. Four centuries immediately after the war set the tone. In 1923 Harry's aggregate was well over 2,000 runs, making 2 double centuries, his highest score of 203 at Worcester and another double century against Northamptonshire at Liverpool. Three years later Lancashire won the Championship, the first of three successive

years. It was Harry's best season. His regular opening partner was Charlie Hallows. They were a perfect combination of right-hand and left-hand players, the correct and cautious Makepeace complemented by the more forceful and stylish Hallows. The Championship was in the balance until the last game against Nottinghamshire when Harry transformed himself into a forcing batsman, top scoring with 180 quick runs and an innings of no chances. The Championship came to Old Trafford.

Invited to tour Australia in 1920/21 against Armstrong's brilliant team, Harry played in 4 Test matches and at Melbourne he scored 117 and 54. He was fourth in the tour averages but Hobbs and Sutcliffe kept him out of more English Tests.

The last of Harry's 43 centuries came on his forty-eighth birthday although, appointed assistant coach to J.T. Tyldesley the previous year, old 'Shakes' kept on performing as long as he was selected. He had passed well over 25,000 runs, the fourth highest aggregate in his county's history, and he will probably hold the record as the oldest Lancashire player to score a century at forty-eight years.

After another twenty years as coach, he retired at seventy years of age. Setting an example of honest play in all his sports, he is remembered fondly as a courteous, knowledgeable player who was an astute judge of cricketers.

Born: Oldham, 31.03.1936

Matches: 236

Batting:

Runs	HS	Av	100s
10,312	142*	29.2	10

Bowling:

Wkts	Av	BB
109	37.7	5-46

Catches: 200

Oldham-born Peter Marner was the youngest player to represent his county, only sixteen years five months when he made his debut at Hove in 1952. He had played for his league side Crompton at fifteen years of age. A thick-set and powerful middle-order right-hand batsman, he scored over 17,000 first-class runs in his career. An accurate seam bowler, just over medium pace, he accumulated 360 wickets and took 379 catches, many of those in the slips where he built his reputation as a fine fielder. One of the hardest hitters of the ball in the game, he was a pugnacious batsman scoring quickly in all forms of cricket.

Peter was the first player ever to win a Man of the Match award in the first one-day Gillette Cup game at Old Trafford in 1963. Lancashire beat Leicestershire in that limited-overs match played before any of the other counties had tried the new format. The great Frank Woolley presented him with the gold medal.

An all-round sportsman, he played rugby union for Oldham at sixteen years of age. He also played for the Army while spending his national service in the Royal Signals as well as cricket for the combined services. He then joined Broughton Park, a premier Lancashire rugby club. It was there that he suffered a serious knee injury which ended his rugby career. Missing the whole of the 1957 cricket season because of it, he came back to play for Lancashire the following year and headed the batting averages with the first 1,000 runs he had achieved in 12 seasons. His best spell of bowling was 5 for 46 against Nottinghamshire at Liverpool in 1962, when he proved to be a valuable all-rounder, taking over 50 wickets alongside his 1,500 runs. He topped the Lancashire batting averages again the following season, making his top score of an unbeaten 142 against Leicestershire at Old Trafford.

In 1965 Peter moved to Leicestershire for 6 seasons after dramatic changes on the Lancashire Committee which resulted in three players leaving. He continued to hit aggressively with explosive innings in all competitions and reached 1,000 runs in all but one of those seasons at Leicestershire. He led the county when Illingworth was absent. Under the captaincy of Richie Benaud he was selected to tour with Commonwealth party in Pakistan in 1968.

Although still in prime form at thirty-four years of age, he gave notice that he did not wish to play county cricket and retired from the first-class game to play league cricket for Todmorden, and later had a short spell at Kearsley. He was injured again playing cricket and ran a pub for a few years before starting a business providing food for larger inns in Lancashire.

In 1993 he managed the Conservative Club at Timperley, retiring at sixty-five years. A family man still living in Oldham, he takes a keen interest in his grandson, an all-rounder for Rochdale youth team. He is still a good golfer and visits Old Trafford to remember old times with his colleagues.

Peter Martin

RHB & RFM, 1989-present

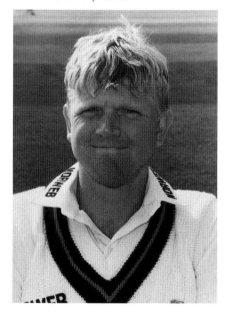

Born: Accrington, 15.11.1968

Matches: 194

Batting:

Runs	HS	Av	100s
3,399	133	20.6	2

Bowling:

Wkts	Av	BB
574	27.1	8-32

Catches: 49

Tests: 8

Peter made his first-class debut at twenty years against the Australians at Old Trafford, opening the bowling with West Indian Pat Patterson. His first first-class wicket was Dean Jones, caught Hegg, a statistic to be repeated many times.

A medium-fast right-hand bowler, he was able to swing the ball away from the right-hand batsman. At 6ft 5ins there is pace and bounce with consistent accuracy, the ingredients of a good fast bowler. But he doesn't possess the expected characteristics of a fast bowler, being calm and easy-going and having a pleasant, humble and amusing nature. He is a gentle giant, a considerate, benevolent man. The only hint of aggression appears when his bowling is hit. A disgruntled figure disturbs the dusty surface with an angry sweeping side kick, annoyed with himself for not hitting the intended spot on the pitch. Like an admonished senior prefect, he turns from his longish walk to attack again and pump those long legs and arms, finishing with a text-book action and perfect line.

In 1995 he was selected to play for England in the one-day international against the West Indies at The Oval. Taking 4 wickets for 44, including bowling Brian Lara, he was awarded Man of the Match. Peter went on to play 19 more one-day matches for England. The same year he was called up to play in his maiden Test match at Headingley, the West Indian captain Richie Richardson being his first victim. Peter toured South Africa with England in June 1995 and played in the World Cup in India and Pakistan. His Lancashire team carried on their one-day trophy success with the Benson & Hedges Cup and NatWest Trophy at Lord's in 1996.

'Digger' Martin (nicknamed after a Dallas television character) joined an exclusive club of ten other Lancashire bowlers who have taken 500 wickets in the last fifty years, as well as over 250 limited-overs wickets. His best spell of bowling was at Uxbridge in 1997 when he took 8 for 32 against Middlesex.

One of the best lower-order batsmen in the country, Digger struck the ball hard. With a long reach and straight bat he was good enough to score 2 centuries and a few fifties, achieving a total of well over 3,000 runs for his county.

Peter is a great ambassador for Lancashire cricket. A caring, generous man, he gave a large part of his successful benefit to research into cancer, the disease that took his mother. Digger enjoys the finer qualities in life, good wine and gourmet food, classical music, but his favourite pastime is painting in oils and watercolour. His originals have attracted much attention. Looking to the future, he is studying for a qualification in management.

Gehan Mendis
RHB & RM, 1986-93

Born: Colombo, 24.04.1955

Matches: 160

Batting:

Runs	HS	Av	100s
9,815	203*	38.9	18

Catches: 54

Gehan Mendis possessed a driving ambition and the confidence to succeed in first-class cricket when he moved to Lancashire in 1986 and capped the same year. He was born in Sri Lanka thirty years earlier and came to Brighton as a twelve-year-old. He was naturalised British when he was twenty-four, turning down invitations to captain the country of his birth. At Durham University he earned a degree in maths and returned to Sussex where he played over 200 first-class matches.

Lancashire were short of a solid, reliable opening batsman and Mendis had proved his quality by scoring over 11,000 runs for his former country. He had quick eyes and nimble feet. His technique was front foot in defence but his quick footwork enabled him to play the short ball effectively. A recognised performer against pace, he had the temperament to attack the fast bowler; the quicker the speed the more he rose to the challenge. In judging his ability we look at the quality of bowling he faced. It compared with the best in any era, including Malcolm Marshall against whom he scored 3 centuries in a row. There was focused concentration and application. Superb against spin too, he displayed a variety of shots around the wicket when facing the left-arm spin of Shastri at his peak. It was not a fleeting performance as he consistently hit 1,000 runs a season and for Lancashire almost 10,000 runs in 8 seasons with a highest score of 203 not out against Middlesex at Old Trafford. It was the first ever double century for Lancashire against

that county. Few batsmen have scored a total of 20,000 first-class runs since the war as well as over 8,000 limited-overs competition runs in a career.

A good player can adapt and succeed in any form of cricket and Mendis scored centuries in all types of competitions, winning 4 NatWest Man of the Match awards and 5 Benson & Hedges gold awards. As an example, he scored a brilliant unbeaten century against Middlesex at Old Trafford in the semi-final of the NatWest Cup in 1990. Playing the sheet anchor, he kept the scoreboard moving swiftly along and watched Atherton, Fowler, Fairbrother Watkinson and Akram all go. This gutsy opening bat showed his true craftsmanship at work, pushing the score past the huge target of almost 300. In first-class cricket his opening partnership with Graeme Fowler was one of the most successful in the country.

This fine player had much knowledge and advice to offer young cricketers but coaching was not his forte. His speciality as an opening batsman was his calling. At the top of his form he should have represented his country. He was superior to some who were called. No other role in cricket seemed to interest him. He retired from the game to join the financial world full-time where his quick mathematical mind would be further challenged.

Born: Middleton Cheney, 27.05.1863
(d. 29.04.1921)

Matches: 260

Batting:

Runs	HS	Av
1,675	57	7.1

Bowling:

Wkts	Av	BB
1,543	15.1	9-29

Catches: 104

Tests: 3

Standing a full six feet tall with piercing eyes, square-chinned and with a full moustache, Arthur was an imposing presence. All batsmen in his day feared the deadliest of fast deliveries from him. He was certainly quick, but the fairness of his action formed the subject of lively discussion in the last few years of his first-class career.

Mold's figures were very impressive over his thirteen-year career for Lancashire. His total of 1,673 wickets is the third highest in the county lists and at an average of 15.5 per wicket proves impressive bowling. Pitches were generally poor in the late nineteenth century and often favoured the bowler. In his day he was recognised as the most destructive bowler in English cricket and at the end of his career he had taken more wickets than any other fast bowler in the world. He had a natural, easy action and bowled with accuracy of length and line and produced movement off the pitch, a combination which brought him immediate success.

The impact of his excellent debut season for Lancashire in 1889 brought instant recognition throughout England. One hundred wickets in his first season at 11.8 and third in the professional bowling averages sent tongues

wagging round the counties. Early in his first season he captured 11 Kent wickets at Old Trafford and was chosen to play against Yorkshire at Huddersfield. In their final innings, Yorkshire required only 75 to win and Mold took 7 for 35 to help Lancashire win by 3 runs. Mold's impressive start was one of the reasons Lancashire shared the Championship with Nottinghamshire and Surrey.

Arthur Mold took 100 wickets in a season nine times, going on to 200 wickets twice. In the first of those two amazing seasons his 207 wickets included a spell against Somerset of 20 balls, no runs and 7 wickets including a hat-trick. Briggs and Mold took 324 Lancashire wickets between them at around 13 runs apiece and not a single county scored 300 runs in an innings against them. On 143 occasions Mold took 5 wickets in an innings and in 14 matches he captured 13 wickets or more in a game. He was chosen for 3 Test matches against Australia in 1893.

Against Nottinghamshire at Trent Bridge in his twelfth season, umpire Jim Phillips no-balled him from square leg. The following season the same umpire called him 16 times in a match. No other umpire judged his action unfair. He dropped out of first-class cricket soon afterwards, playing league-cricket in his native Northamptonshire, going shooting, running a pub and looking after his aged mother. His prolific record remains.

Muttiah Muralitaran
RHB & OB, 1999-2001

Born: Kandy, 17.04.1972

Matches: 14

Batting:

Runs	HS	Av
100	21	6.6

Bowling:

Wkts	Av	BB
116	15	7-39

Catches: 6

Tests: 85

There may be frowned brows questioning the inclusion of a cricketer who has played only 14 games for Lancashire to date, but a very special cricketer he is. Murali reached 100 wickets in his twelfth match. He is the quickest to this mark by any bowler in the history of cricket. This spinning wizard deserves to be included even at this early stage of his Lancashire career. His ambition is to pass 600 Test wickets.

Murali has extravagant wrist-driven action; every muscle in his arm assists the viciousness of the spinning ball. After a short run-up, there is direction concentration on variation of pace, of line and spin. The ball can dip quickly and deceptively and the variety of attack includes a startling top-spinner shooting straight on and lifting. His stock ball is the off-break, pushed through at pace and turning quickly with the occasional googly obscured by speed of twirling wrist. A bowler of great quality, he is constantly looking to improve his phenomenal success. Working on a curving ball which swings in to the left-handed batsman, he is practising that skill with the ball spinning back the other way. It is almost unplayable if he adds this to his varied attack.

At 5ft 5ins tall, he has a round, homely face full of smiles with a mischievous twinkle in his dark brown eyes. He is very competitive with a Scrooge-like attitude to giving away runs. There is a fervour in his play, always encouraging his team mates. He is warmly welcomed in the dressing room and fits in like a son of Accrington.

His prodigious turn comes from a wrist action that was developed to overcome deformation in the right arm. It is perfectly fair but appears different. He was called for throwing by two Australian umpires. The ICC and experienced Test bowlers studied video evidence when he was filmed over a period from twenty-seven different angles. The judgement was that his action was legal. Don Bradman's opinion was that the umpires had made an error, Murali was a wondrous talent, he said. Through all this, the bowler remained patient, mentally strong with dignified silence.

After taking 14 wickets in a Test against England, Lancashire moved quickly to invite him to play as their overseas cricketer. Arriving in June 1999, this delightful, small man with youthful frame took 66 wickets in 7 matches including the first, although it was rain-affected and he didn't bowl. His first bowling stint captured 14 Warwickshire wickets, then 10 against Surrey, 13 against Essex and 10 against Glamorgan. Two years later in a part season of 7 matches (due to Sri Lanka calling on his valued services once more) he performed more wizardry, taking 50 wickets. His total of 116 wickets for his county cost only 15 runs each.

Members who have been privileged to witness this exceptional bowler will want him to be mentioned with Lancashire's best.

Norman 'Buddy' Oldfield

RHB, 1935-39

Born: Dukinfield, 05.05.1911 (d. 19.04.1996)

Matches: 151

Batting:

Runs	HS	Av	100s
7,002	147*	35.7	12

Bowling:

Wkts	Av	BB
2	42.5	1-0

Catches: 32

Tests: 1

A neat cricketer, small in stature with a full head of black hair, he would sit at the window, padded up, staring out to the middle with deep-set eyes. A man of most nervous disposition, he was a constant smoker and his habitual facial twitches and incessant blinking became well known. Seldom did he eat a meal before batting for fear of vomiting. Once at the crease, nerves subsided and we saw a fine stroke-maker, mostly off the back foot, fearlessly pulling and hooking. He was a devastating cutter and his exquisite timing completed his qualities as a gifted batsman.

Popularly known as 'Buddy' from the time he arrived at Old Trafford as a young professional in 1929, it took him six years before he made his first team debut. Lancashire had won the Championship the previous year with a strong, powerful side and Buddy's slight, 5ft 5ins figure may have counted against him. His determination, attractive play and consistent scoring persuaded the club to select him and he rewarded them with 1,000 runs each season up to the interruption of war.

Buddy soon made his maiden century in his first season against Hampshire at Liverpool and another unbeaten century followed at Old Trafford two weeks later. Against the touring Indians at Old Trafford the following year he shared a stand of over 200 with Cyril

Washbrook in two hours twenty minutes, both making centuries but Buddy playing the more attractive cricket. Eddie Paynter and he held the 3rd wicket partnership record of 306 at Southampton and it remained the best for over fifty years.

Consistent high scoring attracted the England selectors and Buddy represented his country in the Final Test against the West Indies at The Oval. He made a brilliant 80 in the first innings, scoring freely with delightful late cuts and well-timed leg glances and drives both sides of the wicket. Outscoring Hutton, Hammond and Compton, the selectors told him he had a promising England career ahead. Then the war broke out twelve days later.

Resuming his career after a six-year break, he believed the salary at Lancashire was insufficient to bring up a family of three boys and Buddy became the landlord of a Lancashire inn until Northamptonshire offered him better terms. Playing there until 1954 he broke the 1st wicket partnership record with Vince Broderick, making 361 against Scotland. He scored a total of almost 18,000 first-class runs in his career.

For ten years he served as an excellent first-class umpire, standing in 2 Test matches before returning to Old Trafford as coach until his retirement in 1972. Buddy was an astute assessor of a player even later in his life when he still twitched and sparkled with enthusiasm when talking and reminiscing about cricket.

Cec Parkin

RHB, OB & LB, 1914-26

Born: Egglescliffe, 18.02.1886 (d. 15.06.1943)

Matches: 157

Batting:

Runs	HS	Av
1,959	57	12

Bowling:

Wkts	Av	BB
901	16.1	9-32

Catches: 107

Tests: 10

The young Cecil Parkin was a thin, wiry, handsome man, a conjurer and prince of jokers who played cricket for fun. For two years he practised his spinners on his long suffering wife, her fingers black from bruising as she courageously stood like an effigy in front of stumps in her persuaded role of imitative batsman. He played one game for Yorkshire before they discovered he was born in County Durham. Lancashire spotted his talents when playing for Church in the Lancashire leagues.

Batting for Lancashire at Lord's with Dick Tyldesley, the two found themselves at the same end of the wicket. The ball was hurled at the deserted wicket and went for overthrows. The grateful and jubilant Parkin shouldered his bat and marched down the pitch singing *The British Grenadiers*. He regularly drew a disapproving frown from the establishment. A well-known comedian on and off the field, he could talk almost as well as he could bowl and was constantly communicating with the crowd, entertaining them by conjuring the ball out of his pocket or performing tricks, flicking the ball in the air with his boots and catching it behind his back. He loved the repartee and response from the supporters.

His eccentric behaviour and constant chatting on the field was tolerated because of his exceptional skills as a right-arm spin bowler. Delivering six different types of ball in an over, he included off-breaks, leg-breaks, high-flighted looping slower balls and fast top-spinners. He varied flight and pace, making it difficult to set

a reliable field. His debut against Leicestershire brought him 14 wickets in the match for 99 runs. Heading the county bowling averages he managed only 6 first-class matches in 1914 as he remained loyal to his weekend commitments in the leagues where the earnings were more lucrative. However he realised that the more authoritarian county game would give him status and a wide reputation so he could demand more salary from a top league side.

Returning to Old Trafford after the wasted war years, he headed the bowling averages once more and produced a 14-wicket haul against Yorkshire at Old Trafford, beating them by 140 runs and outshining Rhodes and Hirst. He played mid-week only for Lancashire, preferring to keep his contract with the league club where his pay was high.

In 1920 he was chosen for the Players match at The Oval and dismissed 9 Gentlemen in the first innings for 85, 6 of whom he clean-bowled. This and other successes persuaded the selectors to take him to Australia in the winter. Playing in all 5 Test matches, he took more wickets than any other England bowler in those Tests and in all matches. A match ball was presented to him from that series, which is exhibited in the Lancashire museum. The leather can be seen to be stud-marked where he constantly flipped the ball up with his boots. The following summer he took 5 for 38 for England against Australia at Old Trafford. Cec was now enjoying his England status, playing in the leagues but still turning out for Lancashire in half a dozen games and representing the Players against the Gentlemen. His decision to play full-time county cricket in 1922 for the next four seasons brought Parkin huge success. He took 189 first-class wickets in the season, averaging 17 runs per wicket, an eye-catching statistic for selectors. He worked hard for his success, bowling over 1,300 overs in the summer.

The following season, his increased experience at first-class level had sharpened his skills and he captured 209 first-class wickets at an average of 16, the highlight being 15 wickets in the match against Glamorgan at Blackpool. He was opening the bowling for his county regularly, being their main bowler. The following season he repeated his 200-wicket success at a meaner average of 13. His first game was for England against the Rest as a Test trial where he took 6 wickets in the match. But it was for Lancashire where he gained most headlines. Six times he took 10 or more wickets in a match and against Leicestershire dismissed 9 batsmen in the second innings for 32 runs, the odd batsman being run out to spoil his record of all 10.

Cec Parkin produced exceptional figures during the season, but they tended to be against weaker counties. However, there was a most remarkable match against Yorkshire at Headingley when the home side only required 57 runs to win with all 10 wickets standing. Dick Tyldesley and Cec Parkin bowled them out for 33 in an astonishing second innings. Cec also took 8 South African wickets for Lancashire at Old Trafford in a most satisfying summer.

In 1925 Cec Parkin was thirty-nine years of age and tiring in his effort to keep bowling 1,000 overs each summer. He managed 152 wickets with an average of 19 and watched the younger McDonald capture his first 200 wickets. Cec enjoyed a benefit match against Middlesex and took home a healthy £1,180 at the end of the summer. This was on top of a very successful benefit from the leagues four years earlier.

The following season was his last in first-class cricket and he ceased to play after the fourteenth game. He had taken 1,048 first-class wickets and played in 10 Test matches. The eminent Jack Hobbs described him at his peak as the best bowler in England. When coaching, Charlie Hallows said he was the best he had seen in his fifty years in cricket.

Outspoken and opinionated, his colourful disagreements with the authorities had influenced the end of his first-class career. He returned to the lucrative leagues and built a successful business in Blackpool where he doubled his weight in an easy lifestyle. He died in a Manchester hospital at fifty-seven years. His son Reg turned out for Lancashire in 20 games as an all-rounder but was never a match for his father's versatility and brilliance as one of Lancashire's most successful bowlers.

Eddie Paynter

LHB & RM, 1926-45

Born: Oswaldtwistle, 05.11.1901
(d. 05.02.1979)

Matches: 293

Batting:

Runs	HS	Av	100s
16,555	322	41.5	36

Bowling:

Wkts	Av	BB
24	52	3-13

Catches: 131

Tests: 20

Born within the heart of Lancashire League cricket at Oswaldtwistle, Eddie joined Enfield Cricket Club where his father was captain of the Second XI. Some months after starting work at the Enfield brick and tileworks he lost the ends of both first and second fingers on his right hand tending a brick press. The hope of being a spin bowler had disappeared. His batting talent attracted the Lancashire coach who invited Eddie to Old Trafford. His debut came in 1926 but it was 1930 before he established his place, playing 15 matches and averaging 25 in a year when the First XI won the Championship. His first century came the following year against Warwickshire and was scored in just two hours. He had opened with Frank Watson occasionally and he was astonished to be selected for the Third Test against New Zealand at Old Trafford, opening with Herbert Sutcliffe. The following year the All India team played their first Test in England at Lord's and Eddie made 50 in the second innings batting with Jardine. The same season Eddie performed his best innings, in his opinion, at Bradford in a Roses game. Whitsun holiday brought the huge crowds and Lancashire batted first on a sticky wicket where few players found it difficult to survive. Crowds witnessed Paynter hitting Bill Bowes and Macauley all over the field in a great display of driving and pulling which lasted three and a half hours. He hit the great Hedley Verity for 3 sixes over the stand into Park Avenue and was finally dismissed for 152 helping his team to win by an innings.

Eddie Paynter was a left-handed batsman, less than 5ft 6ins in height and about ten and a half stones in weight. He had great natural ability, possessing all the shots around the wicket. An attacking batsman who could drive a ball superbly, he was also an excellent cutter and hooker. Many of his runs were scored with his famous pull to the leg side and he could delicately late cut and hit the best of bowlers over the fielders to the boundary. He had quick feet and was particularly effective against slow bowlers. He never worried about attempting to read the spin, his movement was quick enough to play the turn from the pitch. Unorthodox in style, he was difficult to contain when in form and bruised the finest of bowlers. His aggressive off-drive was executed on occasions with both feet off the ground. There was also a stubborn defence when required. An innings by him may show a mixture of obstinacy and belligerence. Always a fighter, he became a difficult wicket to claim. The England captain, Jardine, admired this determined Lancastrian and Eddie was selected for the famous bodyline tour of Australia.

It was on this trip that he acquired international respect and celebrity status. At Brisbane, England's batting was in trouble and the Ashes series at risk. Eddie had been taken to hospital with tonsillitis and was listening to the commentary of the Test match on the wireless. As wickets were falling, he decided to rejoin his team and against condemnations and remonstrations from the medical staff, still in his pyjamas, dressing gown and slippers, he left his hospital bed, took a taxi to the ground and went out to bat. His temperature was high and in the heat of the Brisbane sun he donned a large panama hat for protection. England were 216 for 6 when he joined the surprised Les Ames at the wicket. At the end of the day Eddie was 24 not out and returned to hospital. Continuing his innings the following day he went on to score 83, a fighting innings that took almost four hours. In the second innings he hit a six to win the match and regain the Ashes.

Returning to England, the Lancashire club insisted on celebrating his great achievements but Eddie, the most modest of Lancastrians, wanted no fuss. He gave the museum one of his prized mementos, a cotton handkerchief presented to him from his Sunday school; printed on it was the Brisbane score.

In 1938 at Trent Bridge he scored an unbeaten 216 in five hours and twenty minutes in the drawn Ashes game. He shared in two record partnerships in that series against Australia. In the Lord's Test he came in to bat with England at 31 for 3 and made a stand of 222 with Wally Hammond for the 4th wicket. His second record partnership was 206 for the 5th wicket with Denis Compton at Trent Bridge. In all Test matches against Australia he averaged 84, the highest for any English batsman in the Ashes history. When he was almost thirty-eight years old he scored 653 runs in the 5 Tests against South Africa, averaging 81. His highest score was 243 in the Third Test at Durban. In the 20 Test matches he played before the war curtailed his career, he scored 1,540 runs with an average of 59.2.

At Old Trafford in July 1937 he played in a Test match against New Zealand and set off on the midnight train to play for his county the next day against Sussex. He arrived in Brighton at eight o'clock in the morning just in time for breakfast before walking to the Hove ground. Opening the innings with Cyril Washbrook, Eddie Paynter scored the highest total ever by a Lancashire professional. In that first day he hit 322 runs with ferocious driving and pulling, reaching a hundred before lunch.

His spectacular hitting lasted five hours with 39 fours and 3 sixes. The game was won by an innings.

Many other records were set during his career. The same year as his triple century, he scored 266 opening against Essex and achieved a new 8th wicket record with Pollard. He gave no chances and players applauded his powerful drives and neat leg glances. He scored 2,904 first-class runs averaging 58 in 1937 having made over 2,000 the previous season. The following year Eddie was chosen as one of Wisden's cricketers of the year and the following season he was asked to captain the Players v. Gentlemen.

The war cut short many great cricketers' careers. In 1946, Eddie decided he was too old for the rigours of first-class cricket even though he was promised a benefit. Instead he received an *ex gratia* award of £1,078. Paynter had scored over 20,000 first-class runs averaging 42. He was an excellent fielder and a superb thrower with safe hands taking 160 catches. Although a part-time bowler he captured 30 wickets with his medium right-arm seam bowling. After retirement he played in two festival games at Harrogate scoring 154, 73 and 127, the latter in 85 minutes.

Finding employment was difficult after the war. He worked in various pubs as well as building sites and cricket coaching roles when he could find them. He was invited to coach cricketers on a trip to India with the Commonwealth team in 1950. Paynter became a first-class umpire for a short time. Before he did he managed to visit Australia for the Centenary Test in 1977 with other Lancashire Test players and he would watch his county whenever someone would take him – he had no car. His wise values and competitive character was formed in the friendly mill towns in east Lancashire where he irked out a modest living, never realising his greatness or the immense pleasure he gave to those to saw him or read about him. Washbrook believed no other Lancastrian could stand in his shadow. No one was more dedicated to the Lancashire cause. Neville Cardus said Paynter batted with a Lancashire accent and character. Many members now sit in the Eddie Paynter stand and in moments of quiet play reflect on the great man's influence on this great club.

Eddie Phillipson
RHB & RFM, 1933-48

Born: Reddish, 03.12.1910 (d. 24.08.1991)

Matches: 158

Batting:

Runs	HS	Av	100s
4,050	113	25.9	2

Bowling:

Wkts	Av	BB
545	24.7	8-100

Catches: 81

When he was a shop assistant with the Co-operative store, Eddie joined Flixton Cricket Club. They recommended him to the county club and when he reached the age of twenty he joined the grounds staff, making his debut the following season. His attraction to Lancashire was his medium-fast right-arm bowling. Eddie was a tall, slim player who was quick, could move the ball off the seam with occasional bounce and was consistently accurate. Against him was that extra yard of speed and a few lapses in health – he dislocated a collar bone on one occasion. He was not the strongest of bowling partners for the sturdy workaholic Dick Pollard, although he was about the same speed.

In his debut game, skipper Peter Eckersley witnessed first hand the usefulness of Eddie's straight batting as they put on over 100 runs together for the last wicket stand. In 1934 Lancashire won the Championship, Eddie playing only a few matches including 8 for 100 at Dover in Kent's first innings. It was difficult breaking into a Championship side but his bowling was too good for the Second XI taking 49 wickets at an average of 8 runs per wicket. The following season he became a more regular opening partner with Pollard and increased his first-class haul to 62 wickets. Beginning to prove his all-round skills, he scored 70 runs and took 5 wickets in the match at Southampton. Good sound batting giving few chances, he was a regular 6 or 7 batsman.

More mature and experienced in 1937, he scored 866 runs and took 131 wickets in first-class cricket averaging 23. There is little doubt that he would have achieved the double had his career not been interrupted. In a match against Nottinghamshire that season, he scored a faultless century with delightful square cuts and cover drives. Even the highly rated Harold Larwood was unable to dismiss him, and the Nottinghamshire man was his role model. Eddie was immediately given the ball and took 5-89 in Nottinghamshire's first innings, clean-bowling his idol. He repeated his near-miss double in 1939, when he achieved a top score of 113 at Preston and the following game took 12 wickets against Kent. Then came that long war break.

Chosen for the unofficial Victory Test at Old Trafford in 1945 he took 6 for 58 and when first-class cricket restarted he was in his thirty-sixth year. His 555 first-class wickets and over 4,000 runs in such a short career was a proud record. He retired from Lancashire to stand in 12 Test matches as a respected umpire and eventually ran a sports business two or three miles from Old Trafford.

Harry Pilling

RHB & OB, 1962-80

Born: Ashton-under-Lyne, 23.02.1943

Matches: 323

Batting:

Runs	HS	Av	100s
14,841	149*	32.2	25

Bowling:

Wkts	Av	BB
1	195	1-42

Catches: 85

Looking a very youthful sixteen years, Harry arrived at Old Trafford after leaving Ashton-under-Lyne technical school. Less than 5ft 3ins tall, life bestowed no favours on him. Everything he achieved he fought for and he thrived on dedication and pressure. He learnt his trade in the leagues at Oldham where they praised him for his skill, courage and composure as the smallest player in the league. He turned his physique to his advantage with quick footwork and wristy shots to compensate for any lack of reach. The secret was his timing: particularly strong on the on-side, he played shots with power and style. Courageous against the quick bowlers, he was also an excellent player of spin.

Harry's maiden century was made at Portsmouth when he was twenty years old and soon he was reaching the 1,000-runs mark regularly. When Clive Lloyd arrived there were many memorable partnerships between the two contrasting players. Batting together against Gloucestershire at Old Trafford they scored a century each in 1970, one of Harry's most successful years. The next game at home, the little giant scored an unbeaten century in each innings against Warwickshire, the first time this feat had been achieved since Washbrook and Place in 1947.

1970 was a successful year for Lancashire, as they won the John Player League, Harry averaging 52 in the competition. He won Man of the Match in the final at Lord's to help his county win the Gillette Cup that year.

Like fine wine, he got better with age, topping the county averages six years later with 1,500 runs averaging 53. At Liverpool he reached his highest score, an unbeaten 149, to set up an easy victory against Glamorgan including a partnership of 290 with Barry Wood. 'Henry' as the dressing room called him, was a regular No.3 bat, reliable and solid in that crucial position in all types of cricket.

Invited to join a Commonwealth XI to tour Pakistan in January 1970, he made two more tours abroad, with an unofficial World XI three years later to Pakistan and a tour to Sri Lanka with D.H. Robins. A place in the England team should have been offered with such a consistent scoring record of over 15,000 first-class runs as well as almost 4,000 limited-overs runs.

When international bowlers Lever, Shuttleworth and Clive Lloyd couldn't take a Somerset wicket at Old Trafford in the early 1970s, Harry came on to bowl and dismissed all-rounder Peter Robinson, his only first-class wicket.

Most spectators could identify with Harry Pilling, never one of the sparkling and explosive big stars but a man of the people, a humble, reliable match winner and very popular cricketer. He had no training for a role outside cricket and he tried his hand at any trade including working as an apprentice butcher, coalman, coffin maker, part of the leisure industry and finishing on shift work in a plastics factory. He was grateful he had a job and could buy a pint. His daughter, proud of father's achievements named her son Harry.

Richard Pilling

RHB & WK, 1877-89

Born: Bedford, 05.07.1855 (d. 28.03.1891)

Matches: 177

Batting:

Runs	HS	Av
1,854	78	10.7

Catches: 333

Stumpings: 153

Tests: 8

In his prime Dick Pilling wrote that a wicket-keeper must possess patience, perseverance, coolness and a certain degree of fearlessness. He agreed that a keeper must be tough, hawk-eyed and swivel-kneed with all joints well oiled and supple. We know that he faced a wider variety of bowling than today with underarm, roundarm and overarm deliveries coming through to him on unreliable pitches. The direction from pitch was more difficult to judge and there was some wild throwing from fielders on returning the ball.

W.G. Grace, the champion cricketer of his day, was not known to give praise generously, but he wrote that Pilling was one of the most brilliant wicketkeepers the world had ever seen. He was without a rival as stumper for six or seven years and his exclusion from a Players' team against good opposition could not be entertained. Dick was quiet, unostentatious, and took the fastest of bowling with consummate ease and astonishing quickness. He crouched over the wicket, his nose close to the bails, snapping the ball with unerring certainty. Wearing little protection with insufficient and scanty gloves and pads, he stood up to fast or spin bowling. The Lancashire pace attack included the fast dangerous deliveries of Crossland. For him he added more padded protection. A.G. Steel was a first-rate leg-spinner on pitches where the ball flew and lifted on unpredictable surfaces. Pilling averaged almost 4 victims a match throughout his career, stumping 206 first-class victims and catching 461 batsmen.

Making his Lancashire debut in 1877 against Sussex at Old Trafford, Dick's first victim was the younger of the Phillips brothers, who was stumped from the bowling of Alex Watson, the slow round-arm Lancashire bowler. He had qualified for the county by playing at Church Cricket Club in the Lancashire leagues. Later he played for the Broughton Club in Manchester and was engaged at Lord's for periods when Lancashire had no matches. The practice improved his own skills but his agility, patience, control and vision proved to be valuable coaching attributes for aspiring wicketkeepers.

Representing England in 8 Test matches from 1881 to 1888, he made two tours of Australia. He is immortalized in the famous stained glass window with Hornby and Barlow which is housed in the Old Trafford Pavilion. All three played in the first Test match at Manchester in 1884. Richard Pilling could stay at the crease on occasions and still holds the 10th wicket partnership record with Johnnie Briggs of 173 at Aigburth, well over 100 years ago.

Still relatively young, he suffered deteriorating health and the Lancashire club paid for his trip to Australia in the winter of 1890/91 hoping he would recover, but he died of consumption a few weeks after his return at the age of thirty-five.

Winston Place

RHB, 1937-55

Born: Rawtenstall, 07.12.1944 (d. 25.01.2002)

Matches: 298

Batting:

Runs	HS	Av	100s
14,605	266*	36.6	34

Bowling:

Wkts	Av	BB
1	42	1-2

Catches: 179

Tests: 3

Like all batsmen with good technique, Winston Place often outlasted his partners on poor pitches. He was a solid, correct player who would calmly raise his cap to acknowledge the crowd on reaching his fifty without any overt gesture. A warm, friendly smile on a pleasant, homely face was all the emotion he showed. Pictures in the mind see him stretching forward in safe defence and then playing a graceful off drive or delighting the crowd with a delicate late cut.

His career, like many others, was interrupted by the war years. Playing for his home town Rawtenstall when he was only fifteen, the great S.F. Barnes was the professional and he told the youngster he had recommended him to Lancashire.

In 1936 he was on the staff and made his debut the following season, scoring his first century at Trent Bridge. He rated the 164 against the West Indies at Old Trafford in 1939 as one of his best innings. After the war the crowds flocked into Old Trafford to see Washbrook and Place open the innings. In 1947 they put on an unbeaten opening stand of 350 against Sussex. Winston in his typical humility wrinkled his face, unable to take praise comfortably, with a suggestion that the bowling was weaker than average.

The consistency of Winston Place was evident in the 1,000 runs he made in each of 8 seasons. He scored 2,400 runs in 1947 averaging nearly 70, including his highest score, an unbeaten 266 against Oxford University in May. He then scored a century in each innings against Nottinghamshire, contributing to a total of 10 centuries in the season. The following winter he was rewarded with a place in the England team visiting the West Indies, where he scored a century in the Test match at Kingston. A year later he was chosen to play in a strong Commonwealth XI to India, Pakistan and Ceylon.

Winston Place scored over 15,600 runs in first-class cricket and after retirement he tried first-class umpiring. Being away from his family didn't suit him so he bought a newsagent's business, playing a little league cricket. Like most players in his era he believes he had the best years in the game. No one who saw him play would argue and disturb the tranquil nature of a delightfully gifted cricketer.

Dick Pollard
RHB & RFM 1933-50

Born: Westhoughton, 19.06.1912

Matches: 266

Batting:

Runs	HS	Av
3,273	63	13.3

Bowling:

Wkts	Av	BB
1,015	22.1	8-33

Catches: 203

Tests: 4

With a strong muscley frame and rustic features, Dick Pollard was one of only ten bowlers to achieve 1,000 wickets for his county. He was born in a village cottage at Daisy Hill and as a youth of fourteen years won bowling, batting and fielding prizes for his Westhoughton Club.

Making his debut for Lancashire in 1933 bowling right-arm medium-fast, his first wicket was the Nottinghamshire and England captain Arthur Carr. His first spell of 21 overs was so accurate that experienced batsmen scored only 36 runs. The following year he took 6 for 21 against Gloucestershire to gain an easy victory. He was eager to bowl all day, seemingly possessing a tireless enthusiasm and boundless energy. He could swing the new ball in the air and cut the old ball off the seam away from the right-handed batsman to make him a dangerous bowler at any level. Pollard would work away patiently until he found a chink in the armour of the most stubborn of batsmen. Ninety per cent of success was hard work, he believed. Nicknamed the 'owd chain horse' for his great heart and perseverance, his accurate deliveries made every batsman work hard for any runs. His most productive season came in 1938 with 149 wickets from over 1,200 overs. At his peak came the Second World War, otherwise he would be challenging the most prolific Lancashire wicket-takers for the highest number of victims. He achieved 100 wickets a season from 1935-47 with the exception of 1946 when he was serving with the Army part of the season.

After impressing in the 'Victory Tests' of 1945, he was chosen to play for England against India, although he was then thirty-four years of age. He took 5 for 24 on his debut at Old Trafford in India's first innings. He went for less than 1 run an over. Bowling for the Players *v*. Gentlemen the same year, he finished the match with figures of 9 for 53.

After touring the MCC to Australia and New Zealand where he played in only 1 Test, he returned to play against Australia in 1948. At Old Trafford he dismissed the great Bradman for 7 runs. The following Test at Leeds he uprooted Bradman's off-stump and 3 balls later dismissed Hassett.

Pollard was granted a benefit in 1949 against Derbyshire which raised over £8,000. After a handful of games the following year he chose to retire and enjoy weekend league cricket in Birmingham and at Preston. He was always a good fielder and could score a quick fifty from the lower order.

Making a success of his small manufacturing company, where he was partner and salesman producing cleaning materials, he was happy in Westhoughton. He continued to entertain people as a competent pianist; in his younger days he had had his own band. Dick and his good pal Bill Farrimond, who lived next door, always kept a tidy garden. There were pedigree dogs too and friendly people around him in his home town.

LHB & RALB 1954-68

Born: Swinton, 01.08.1935

Matches: 312

Batting:

Runs	HS	Av	100s
16,853	167*	35.1	32

Bowling:

Wkts	Av	BB
8	38.1	3-91

Catches: 107

Tests: 28

Joining Werneth Cricket Club in the Central Lancashire League as a youth, Geoff developed a bad habit of backing away in the crease. It was cured when the coach placed large stones behind him. Good scores soon attracted Lancashire coach Stan Worthington who invited Geoff to play in the second XI; a big hundred in only his second appearance confirmed the talent. Driving a little red Triumph sports car, the players nicknamed him 'Noddy'.

There was style and grace in his tall left-hander's stroke play. Particularly strong on the front foot, he proved to have a solid, reliable technique against fast bowlers and moved his feet well against the spinners. At twenty years of age he made his maiden century against Derbyshire, which encouraged him to move up the batting order to No.3. The following year he scored 1,000 first-class runs in the season and repeated the feat a further 8 seasons (over 2,000 in 2) topping the Lancashire batting averages in 6 of these.

The England selectors observed his sound technique and calm temperament. He was asked to open the innings in the Third Test against India in 1959. Though he never liked the position he was remarkably successful, scoring 75 on his debut Test, following this with a century in his next, the first Lancastrian to score a Test hundred at Old Trafford. He toured the Caribbean the following winter. No other England batsman played the West Indian pace attack with more ease and assurance. In the following series against the South Africans he made his highest career score of 175 batting with Cowdrey at The Oval. He rates this as his finest innings. Touring India he made a record 2nd wicket partnership of 164 with Barrington and finished with a visit to Australia where Davidson caused him problems. He finished with a Test batting average of over 43.

In 1968 a disagreement with Tommy Higson, the Lancashire chairman, caused his move to Gloucestershire for 2 seasons. Before retiring from first-class cricket he scored 21,538 runs averaging over 35. Fielding wasn't his strongest asset but he took 125 catches and 10 wickets as an occasional leg-break bowler.

He has lived in the idyllic town of Knutsford for over thirty years, trying his hand in the financial world, food outlets, selling sports equipment and driving for a business friend. A warm, honest, friendly man, generous in praise for good cricket, he is always genuinely interested and concerned about the game, offering help and advice to his Lancashire colleagues.

Born: Kirkham, 27.09.1914 (d. 24.08.1951)

Matches: 114

Batting:

Runs	HS	Av
810	51	10.9

Bowling:

Wkts	Av	BB
382	20.8	8-50

Catches: 58

Running in smoothly with a conventional delivery, Bill Roberts bowled accurate left-arm spinners. He was much more conservative on good wickets, bowling a more predictable length, but on drying wickets he became transformed, added resource and variety to spin and length, and bowled with expectation for each delivery. Happiest under these conditions, often prevalent in the English summer, he could destroy a side in a session. He was never unruffled except when chasing a ball on the boundary. Thoroughly enjoying his cricket, his cheerful and unworried approach was popular with team mates who never felt threatened by his presence in the side. The nearest to an outward sign of exhilaration he showed was a single clap and quiet chuckle when he captured a wicket.

Starting his Lancashire career a few months before the Second World War, Bill Roberts showed early promise and was capped. He was demobbed from the Army as a sergeant and returned to his county headquarters having missed the guidance of those crucial early years of development. Natural talent saw him gain national recognition when he was selected to play three 'Victory Test' matches against Australia at Sheffield and Lord's.

The following season he reached 100 wickets with ease, taking 5-wicket hauls against most counties. Among his best performances were 10 wickets in a match to beat Nottinghamshire at Old Trafford, 5 for 23 against Leicestershire and

5 for 18 against Cambridge University. His inspired bowling kept Lancashire in the title chase until the final stages.

One of his most memorable performances came in Cyril Washbrook's benefit game against the Australians. Roberts was fourth change bowler after Lancashire struggled to achieve a breakthrough. The popular left-armer dismissed 6 of the first 7 Australian batsmen including Bradman, for 73. At one point he had taken 5 for 29 against one of the best sides ever to tour England. He was only one short of 100 wickets for the 1948 season.

In a match at Old Trafford, Glamorgan were dismissed by mid-afternoon and Lancashire lost early wickets quickly. Bill Roberts was sent in as nightwatchman to stay with Jack Ikin and, thoroughly enjoying the experience, he hit out to score his only half century. Out, stumped, he trotted back to the pavilion nodding and smiling to the crowd, contented as usual with his contribution.

Strong competition gave him fewer chances but not before his best figures of 8 for 50 (11 in the match) against Oxford University. In 1950 he topped the Second XI bowling averages and received £2,623 for his benefit. A season later he was forced to have a major operation from cancer and tragically died at the early age of thirty-six.

E.B. Rowley

RHB & occas. WK, 1865-80

Born: Manchester, 04.05.1842 (d. 08.02.1905)

Matches: 81

Batting:

Runs	HS	Av
1,626	78	13.2

Catches: 23

Stumpings: 1

The last official bare-knuckle boxing match was fought in England in 1860, resulting in a draw after 42 hard rounds. That year the British Golf Championship started. These events coincided with Edmund Rowley's first-class career. He became Lancashire's first regular captain, a dashing batsman, topping the national averages in 1859, an occasional bowler and an enthusiastic leader.

Schooled at Rossall, he represented the Manchester Cricket Club at the inaugural meeting to form the Lancashire County Cricket Club. As a solicitor in Manchester he served on the county committee, steering the club through the difficult first steps.

There were seven Rowley brothers who were all proficient cricketers. Alexander and his younger brother Edmund succeeded in the first-class game when time allowed. The first matches played under the title of Lancashire County Cricket Club were played in 1864 and at all but one of the 8 matches arranged the club was represented entirely by amateurs. It was a Gentleman's club and a Rowley brother represented the team in every game. The Gentlemen of Lancashire defeated the Gentlemen of Yorkshire home and away, the

brothers Ernest and Alexander taking all second innings wickets between them at York.

In the early years of Lancashire cricket Edmund Rowley pleaded with the great Lancashire-born amateurs who chose to play in only a few matches to represent their county more regularly. E.B. Rowley was partly guilty himself as he played in only 7 of the first 26 away matches. The amateur gentlemen preferred to play at Old Trafford and avoid long, uncomfortable journeys. The problem came to a head in 1871 when most of the amateurs chose to play in a North of England Gentlemen's side against the South. Many untried players turned up for Lancashire and the side lost to Derbyshire, making their lowest score of 25. It is still the lowest Lancashire score.

Edmund worked hard to establish a settled team bringing in gifted amateurs and a regular group of professional bowlers. Results improved and soon Lancashire were a difficult side to beat. Having fulfilled his ambition he resigned the captaincy.

Edmund Rowley's contribution was immense. As a batsman his highest score was a magnificent 219 against the Gentlemen of Yorkshire. But it was his drive and energy and his dedication to the county as an active committee man that helped Lancashire to become a powerful force in the game.

Vernon Royle
RHB & SRA, 1873-91

Born: Brooklands, 29.01.1854 (d. 21.05.1929)

Matches: 74

Batting:

Runs	HS	Av
1,754	81	15.6

Bowling:

Wkts	Av	BB
2	57	1-22

Catches: 34

Tests: 1

Over the lengthy period of Lancashire's history, a string of specialist fielders in the covers have emerged. The first of Lancashire's brilliant cover points was Vernon Royle, whose reputation started when he was at Oxford where he was awarded a blue. His fielding was outstanding in his day, being quick-footed and ambidextrous with a sharp return above the stumps. He had won many races as an athlete at Rossall School, particularly in sprinting, and opposition XIs were aware of his great reputation. In a match against Yorkshire, Royle as usual was patrolling the covers. Tom Emmett's remark to his fellow Yorkshireman who called him for a quick single, 'Woah, mate, there's a policeman', was a typical tribute to his excellent skills.

Although overarm bowling was legal, Vernon Royle preferred round arm bowling: the ball projected from square of the body rather than above it. He was fast at first but later developed a slower ball. In the Universities match at Lord's in 1875 he took 4 for 51 in that style, giving few runs away. Over 25,000 people paid a shilling to watch the game over three days.

Dominated by amateurs, Lancashire invited Vernon Royle to play for the First XI in 1873,

the year lawn tennis as we know it was invented. He had a pleasant batting style with a powerful straight drive and a sound defence. Playing for the Gentlemen of Cheshire the following year, he scored a magnificent 205 against Staffordshire Borderers at Chelford. Second in the Lancashire batting averages 2 seasons later, he was invited to Australia with Lord Harris' team. Against Victoria he was top scorer with 75 and took 5 brilliant catches in the covers. His only Test appearance was in the Melbourne game in January 1879, only the third Test match in the history of the game.

Vernon Royle became a master at Elstree school in his mid-twenties. While holding that position he was ordained and served some years as curate of Aldenham near Watford. Eventually head of the school, he transferred his role to Stanmore Preparatory School, where he was head until he died at seventy-five years of age. He kept close links with his Lancashire club, being President when he passed away.

Jack Sharp

RHB & LFM, 1899-1925

Born: Hereford, 15.02.1878 (d. 28.01.1938)

Matches: 518

Batting:

Runs	HS	Av	100s
22,015	211	31.1	36

Bowling:

Wkts	Av	BB
434	27.2	9-77

Catches: 231

Tests: 3

Many remarkable achievements were accomplished by this sportsman, who played in every match of a Championship-winning season for Lancashire County Cricket Club, became a double international representing his country at cricket and football, scored a Test century and won an FA Cup final medal. John Sharp played twenty-seven years for Lancashire, captaining his side for three years. He played in two cup finals for Everton as a right-winger, beating Newcastle 1-0 in 1906 at the Crystal Palace and was runner up to Sheffield Wednesday the following year. He played soccer for England, helping them to beat Ireland in 1903 and Scotland in 1905, then the prime fixture.

Lancashire selected the well-known Everton forward as a bowler at first. 'Jack' was a medium-fast left-arm bowler who had a natural capacity for making the ball lift awkwardly. He would deliver the odd ball at extra pace and cut it back into the right-handed batsman with great success. In his third season he took 112 Championship wickets with an average of 22 each. At Worcester he dismissed 9 batsman in the second innings for 77 runs, his career best analysis.

Making his debut against Surrey in 1899, he batted at No.9 and added the highest partnership of the innings, 115 runs with Alex Eccles for the 8th wicket. A sturdy, thick set, smallish right-handed batsman, he could pull with plenty of power and was strong on the off-side with hard punching off drives and proficient, effective cuts. Jack also had a sound defence. He developed into an entertaining player, scoring freely around the wicket. He was on the Liverpool Cricket Club staff at seventeen years, living in the same street as his long-time friend Harry Makepeace. He moved to Leyland Cricket Club where many young Lancashire players were groomed. Lancashire needed a seam bowler, but it became obvious they had taken on an all-rounder. Jack was a brilliant fielder, quick and decisive, particularly at cover point.

His first captain was Archie MacLaren, the positive, gifted aristocratic amateur who influenced Jack's early years. At twenty-five years of age, Sharp's batting ability had been recognised and he made a century before lunch at Old Trafford against Sussex on the third day, batting with Reggie Spooner. The following year, 1904, Lancashire won the Championship, Jack playing in all the games. The team was unbeaten all summer, including matches against the South Africans and the Rest of England. In 1905 he reached his 1,000 runs in the season, a feat he achieved for 10 summers. He was being asked to bowl less frequently, although Jack did take 4 Australian wickets for 27 off 10 overs at Old Trafford. Overall his bowling was becoming more expensive and his batting more reliable. In the Everton Cup winning season of 1906,. Jack scored 1,000 runs with 3 centuries, second in the batting averages even after a long season of football.

In 1908, A.H. Hornby was appointed captain and the following year Lancashire were runners-up to Kent in the Championship. Jack was selected to play for England against Australia, the first player born in Hereford to reach Test level. He played at Headingley, Old Trafford and The Oval, where he took three wickets and scored a century, the only one by an Englishman in the series. He had bowled very well for Lancashire at Lord's against Middlesex, dismissing 6 men in 4 overs and 2 balls finishing with 8-51 as well as being Lancashire's top scorer with 54. For England he batted no lower than No.5, so was looked upon as a genuine all-rounder. His successful football career prevented him taking any MCC tours.

Lancashire awarded him a benefit in 1910 and he chose the Roses game on August Bank Holiday. It was very well attended the first day when Lancashire bowled out Yorkshire in just over two hours. Spooner scored a double century and Lancashire won by an innings. Jack was presented with a healthy £1,679 for his benefit. His best form came in the following season when he scored over 2,000 first-class runs. He opened the bowling at Derby and in 6 overs took 5 wickets for 14 runs. These brilliant bowling spells were becoming less frequent as he was well into his thirties. At his peak as a batsman, he made a record 7th wicket partnership of 245 with his captain Hornby in just two and a half hours against Leicestershire at Old Trafford. A relatively wealthy man after two successful careers in sport, he decided to invest in a sports outfitting business in Liverpool where he was famous and well respected. His future was secure.

After the long interruption of the First World War, Lancashire invited Jack to play in 1919. Although forty-one years of age, it was an attractive proposition just getting back to normality. Jack decided to change status from professional to amateur. He could afford the change and felt free to attend his successful business if required. He often stood in as captain when Myles Kenyon suffered from ill health. Jack was appointed official captain in 1923 and led the side for three years. His appointment encouraged a resurgence in his batting form. He came fourth in the Lancashire averages. The team were successful despite having no bowler quicker than Parkin, an off-break bowler. The untimely death of fast bowler Jim Tyldesley just before the season gave him a real challenge.

There was concern in the Committee Room about how Sharp might deal with the strong and opinionated personalities in the dressing room, but he had achieved so much in sport he was bound to attract respect and admiration from other professionals. He always maintained a bright and cheerful disposition. His unquenchable spirit and charm helped his success and Lancashire finished third twice and fourth in the Championship table during his captaincy. In 1924 he was made Test selector, the first ever who had been a professional cricketer.

He was forty-seven years of age in his last season. Missing a catch, the first ball to the Middlesex batsman who put on a 121-run partnership, resulted in criticism from a few barrackers present. Jack Sharp didn't need the hassle. He was persuaded to stay to the end of the season. He had plenty to do as a director of Everton FC and with a business to run. Jack had made more appearances for Lancashire than any other player except Ernest Tyldesley. He had scored over 22,000 runs for his county, 36 centuries and captured 434 wickets. Lancashire made him an honorary life member of the club.

Born: St Helens, 13.11.1944

Matches: 177

Batting:

Runs	HS	Av
1,929	71	16.4

Bowling:

Wkts	Av	BB
484	22.9	7-41

Catches: 84

Tests: 5

A tall, strongly built, fearsome right-handed bowler, Ken Shuttleworth should have played in more than 5 Test matches. He looked the part, with a textbook action and dangerous away swing.

Born in St Helens, he was an effective bowler at fourteen years and played league cricket with Earlstown at an early age. After a spell with St Helen Recs he was invited to play with the Lancashire Second XI at nineteen years and the following year made his debut in a Roses game. Geoff Boycott was his first victim. He was a genuine fast bowler, some say with a similar style to Fred Trueman. Lancashire had excellent support for Brian Statham with Higgs, Lever and Shuttleworth often competing. In 1968 Ken made his mark with 65 first-class wickets. At Leyton he took 7 for 41, rain foiling his second spell. Two years later he captured 74 wickets averaging just over 21. Ken toured Pakistan with the Commonwealth team in 1967/68 under the captaincy of Richie Benaud.

The moral and political decision to withdraw from the South African Tests brought a strong Rest of the World side to England in 1970. Ken was chosen to play for England at Lord's. He went to Australia with Ray Illingworth's Ashes-winning side and started

his Test career with 5 for 47 at Brisbane where his opening partner in Tests was Peter Lever. The following season he played against Pakistan at Edgbaston.

Lancashire's success in the one-day game around the early 1970s was aided by Shuttleworth's accurate short spells. He took 5 for 13 against Nottinghamshire at Trent Bridge in 1972 including the wicket of Gary Sobers. In limited-overs cricket he took 147 wickets averaging 18.

His best batting performance came in 1967 when he was top scorer in the match with 71 against Gloucestershire. In the second innings he made an unbeaten half century, top scorer again. If the skills are possessed, success in sport depends on confidence and complete self belief. An inexplicable moment can place doubt in the mind and affect performance. One such incident happened against Yorkshire in a few overs at the end of the day. Line and length were erratic, the ball was bouncing twice and going wide; for a short time control was lost. The next day would have solved the problem but it rained. The problem remained on Ken's mind and nagged away at his confidence. Ken joined Leicestershire in 1977 and took another 75 wickets in four years, but he was never as effective as in his early years with Lancashire. Well over 600 first-class wickets at 24 each was a fair contribution to the game.

After a few years in business Ken Shuttleworth returned to the game as a first-class umpire.

Frank Sibbles

RHB, RM & OB, 1925-37

Born: Oldham, 15.03.1904 (d. 20.07.1973)

Matches: 308

Batting:

Runs	HS	Av
3,436	71*	14.8

Bowling:

Wkts	Av	BB
932	22	8-24

Catches: 176

In the Central Lancashire League Frank Sibbles preferred to develop his batting skills, but when he arrived at Old Trafford he quickly discovered that better pitches and longer matches suited his bowling, which consisted of accurate medium-pace in-swingers. He could change his style to slower or quicker than medium if conditions suited but the flight of the ball seldom varied. It was said of him that he was too mechanical, lacking flair to experiment, but he achieved 940 first-class wickets in a thirteen-year career and was a member of 5 Championship sides.

Being a most courteous, well-mannered, gentle, mature cricketer made Frank Sibbles a popular team man. He was homespun rather than aristocratic, obliging and generous rather than aggressive and he had the gift of making everyone feel at ease in his comfortable presence. There was no obvious impulsive or reckless impetuosity shown in the outward behaviour of Frank Sibbles and his patient and tolerant characteristics had many advantages in the art of bowling. His nickname, 'Top', because of his wrinkled hair, seemed to suit the respected personality of the man and be in keeping with his style of play.

He made his debut against Somerset with 6 wickets in the match and finished the season with 43 wickets heading the bowling averages at 13 runs per wicket. The following season he increased his total to help win the first of his

5 Championships. In 1927, he opened the bowling with Ted MacDonald, tearing through the Somerset side with 8 for 24 in the first innings, 12 in the match, to gain the win.

Dick Tyldesley and Ted MacDonald had retired by the 1932 season and Sibbles took over as number one bowler. He responded with 131 wickets at only 18 runs each from well over 1,000 overs. In the match at Bradford he captured 12 Yorkshire wickets in the match, taking 7 wickets for 10 runs from 20 overs in the first innings. His accuracy paid off with 13 maidens. He chose his benefit match against Middlesex at Old Trafford in 1937 receiving £1,229 and achieving another 100 wickets. This was his last season as he developed tennis elbow and retired through the injury.

His devotion to the task and hard work earned him the respect he deserved. He was a good listener and led by example. His upright carriage and handsome appearance suggested a sense of dignity and when war called him to service he rose through the ranks to become a major. Success continued later when he became a partner in a Manchester sports business and moved into a comfortable home in Cheshire.

Jack Simmons

RHB & OB, 1968-89

Born: Accrington, 28.03.1941

Matches: 429

Batting:

Runs	HS	Av	100s
8,773	112	22.6	5

Bowling:

Wkts	Av	BB
985	26.8	7-64

Catches: 325

The most popular of players and devoted to his county, Jack Simmons was a burly, accurate off-spinner and a useful right-hand batsman. He was an amiable, honest, dependable team man who was uncomplicated, loyal to his friends and passionate about Lancashire cricket. He had an undiminished enthusiasm for the game and for years was the lynchpin around which the one-day cup successes were built. His bowling style was to push it through; there was no looping flight. Yorkshire's Jack Nicholson nicknamed him 'Flat Jack', referring to his low trajectory. The ball didn't spin viciously but there was consistent accuracy of line and length. Bowling a succession of Yorkers, the batsmen found it difficult to score quickly and their frustration earned Jack wickets. In total, Jack took 1,033 first-class wickets (plus 464 limited-overs wickets) and scored 9,417 runs (plus over 3,000 in limited-overs). In all types of cricket he became only the second player to make the magic 10,000 runs and 1000 wickets, after Johnnie Briggs.

Jack was born in Clayton-le-Moors close to Great Harwood, where he now lives. At fourteen years of age he played for Enfield Cricket Club like his father and grandfather before him. He made his first-class debut for Lancashire at 27 years, finishing his career as a draughtsman. He had the dexterity to dismiss batsmen and score runs at the right time. The popular limited-overs game brought in crowds and phenomenal success. Lancashire became kings of one-day cricket. They won the Sunday League competition in the first two years, followed by 4 Gillette Cup medals in the early 1970s. Jack played in a total of 9 cup finals at Lord's. His prime value was his effective bowling, but he was a capable batsman too. Batting as nightwatchman at Hove in 1970, he scored an excellent century with fluent strokes all round the wicket.

During six winters the all-rounder played for Tasmania in Australian cricket where his massive influence as coach and captain took the team into the Sheffield Shield and won the Gillette Cup final against Queensland. Jack's all-round outstanding performance won him Man of the Match. He was held in great esteem, almost elevated to nobility by the Australians.

Overlooked as captain for Lancashire, a different committee would have appointed him. There was a steely quality to his outwardly easy-going personality. He proved that in Tasmania. He had shown it in his youth when he led the forward line as part-time professional for Great Harwood FC in the Lancashire combination, a prolific goalscorer for eight years.

Awarded a deserved record benefit in 1980, Jack seemed to improve with time like good wine. He topped the batting and bowling averages when forty-one years old and was chosen as a Wisden cricketer of the year. After retirement he became director of a leisure centre, which he gave up when appointed chairman of Lancashire County Cricket Club.

Born: Bootle, 21.10.1880 (d. 02.10.1961)

Matches: 170

Batting:

Runs	HS	Av	100s
9,889	247	37.1	25

Bowling:

Wkts	Av	BB
5	110	1-5

Catches: 106

Tests: 10

The son of a clergyman who later became Archdeacon of Liverpool, Reggie Spooner was a natural games player. His talent for many sports was evident at Marlborough School where he captained the cricket XI in his last year. Scoring almost 1,000 runs that season and averaging 71 with the bat, he also took 25 wickets as an off-break bowler. His talent was so outstanding that within a month of leaving school he was playing for Lancashire against Middlesex at Lord's. Daily news on the Boer War dominated the media and after an absence of three years fighting, Reggie returned to play in the three-quarters for the England rugby team against Wales at Swansea.

The summer of 1903 arrived and Reggie opened the batting with his captain Archie MacLaren, with J.T. Tyldesley coming in at No.3. It is difficult to think of a more talented first three in England. The opening pair put on a record partnership of 368 against Gloucestershire at Liverpool, still a record 1st wicket score for the county. The same season he scored a magnificent 247 at Trent Bridge, the highest score against Nottinghamshire at that time and the first of 5 double centuries in his career. He was the first Lancastrian to score a hundred before lunch, a feat he repeated on four other occasions. His best season was 1911 when he scored over 2,300 first-class runs averaging 51.

The greatest of stylists, Reggie Spooner was a delight to watch, a dream for the purist spectator. His off-drive was the definition of elegance. A wristy player with exquisite timing, he was incapable of looking awkward. He was equally effective on the back foot as on the front. Photographs from the famous Beldam collection show graceful off-drives with the head held high and full follow through. Reggie's charming style was appreciated by Neville Cardus. His batting, wrote the maestro, 'was all courtesy and breeding' and his strokes across the green would have honoured the lawns of any Royal Palace. Slim, tall and athletic, he was noble in stance and movement, even impeccable at cover point.

Chosen to play for England against the 1905 Australians at Old Trafford, he went on to play a total of 10 Test matches, scoring a century against the South Africans at Lord's in 1912. Reggie was asked to skipper the MCC tour to Australia 1920/21 but injury forced him to withdraw.

Business commitments limited his county appearances throughout his cricket career as an amateur. He was President of the club in 1946/47. History remembers him as the most stylish of all Lancashire players.

Born: Manchester, 17.06.1930 (d. 10.06.2000)

Matches: 430

Batting:

Runs	HS	Av
4,237	62	10.5

Bowling:

Wkts	Av	BB
1,816	15.1	8-34

Catches: 171

Tests: 70

Brian Statham was the most successful bowler in the long history of Lancashire County Cricket Club. He took more wickets for Lancashire than any other player and more England Test match wickets than any other Lancastrian, and headed the bowling averages for 16 seasons, 8 more than any other player. Brian took a total of 2,260 wickets in first-class cricket with an average of 16.3 per wicket. In 1960 he achieved his usual 100 wickets at an average of 10.6. No bowler having taken 2,000 wickets has achieved this overall low average since the First World War.

Brian was the most consistently accurate bowler in the game. There was a natural elasticity in his rhythmic run-up, showing impeccable tuning and balance which produced a whipped action and surprising pace. Cricketers who never saw him play said he was too kind and generous to be a fast bowler. But Brian didn't need to intimidate. It was his persistent accuracy of line and length, of pace and skill that did the necessary damage. Players who witnessed his accuracy suggested that he must have taken many wickets for the bowler at the other end. Freddie Trueman, his England opening partner for many years, must have benefited greatly. 'Oh no,' Brian would say, 'Fred got just as many for me.' He wouldn't hear a word spoken against his best opening

partner. Together they took over 550 Test wickets for their country.

Brian was a most gifted all-round sportsman, a superb tennis player and a talented footballer whose wing-half partner in his youth team was Roger Byrne, who went on to captain Manchester United and England. Brian was offered terms with Manchester United and Liverpool but fortunately his father guided him into the game at which he excelled and 50,000 members and more at Lancashire's Old Trafford are most grateful for the reasoned judgement of a wise father.

Playing for his youth club side Denton West, Brian was invited for trials at the county ground and as he had never seen a live first-class match, he thought he should visit the ground before being offered a playing contract there. His first game for Lancashire was against Kent on his twentieth birthday. Their star player was Arthur Fagg, the Kent and England opening batsman. Lancashire's senior professional was Cyril Washbrook who came to Brian before the start of the game and stated firmly that he didn't want Brian to bowl a bouncer at Arthur Fagg as he could hook the ball successfully to the boundary. The time came for Brian to open the bowling from the Stretford end and the fourth ball he dropped short, a mild bouncer which was too quick for Arthur Fagg, who was caught out at silly mid-on. Instead of running to Brian to congratulate him on dismissing their best batsman and taking his first wicket in county cricket,

Washbrook waved his accusing finger at Brian: 'I thought I told you not to bowl a bouncer at Arthur Fagg!' Brian shrugged his shoulders and answered, 'You didn't tell me who Arthur Fagg was.' Brian didn't know the famous names. Bowling for Lancashire was no different from bowling for Denton West. That was the magical uniqueness of this great bowler. He had so much natural ability that only a few months later he was called up to play for England with his best Lancashire pal Roy Tattersall and went on to head the England averages.

One of his most memorable matches was at Lord's in a Test match against South Africa when he bowled throughout the second innings without a break taking 7 for 39 to gain an unexpected victory for England. At Melbourne in 1958 he took 7 for 57 against a strong Australian side and in 1961 at Old Trafford in an Ashes Test his figures were 5 for 53 from 21 overs when hardly any Australian batsmen managed to play him in the middle of the bat. He became the second England bowler to take 250 wickets in Test matches.

Brian was double-jointed, and he would reach behind his shoulders down his back and pull his sweater up and over his head to hand it to the umpire. It was a unique ritual I have never witnessed before. Washbrook, his Lancashire captain for many years, admired him above any player: 'He was a perfect team member. Never once in the years I played with him did Brian ask for a single over more or show the slightest resentment when taken off or asked to bowl.' On some occasions his boots were soaked in blood from over-worked feet but there was never a complaint. The phenomenal number of wickets he took for Lancashire he captured at an astonishingly low average of 15.1. He was a brilliant fielder and catcher. Batting wasn't his greatest strength but he scored 5 fifties, his highest being 62 in 25 minutes in 1955. 'It was a good, old-fashioned, hearty slog,' he recalled.

In his last match, a Roses game at Old Trafford, he took 6 for 34 in the first innings.

On each and every one of the three days the massive crowd gave him a standing ovation as he entered and left the field of play.

Brian Statham gave a great deal back to cricket, particularly his Lancashire Club. He was President of the Lancashire Schoolboys, giving advice and time to help the young cricketers. Brian served on the Lancashire Committee for twenty-six years. He received many honours: captain of the club for three years, the CBE in 1966, an honorary doctorate from Lancaster University and the highest office of President of the Lancashire County Cricket Club. The Warwick Road end has been re-named Brian Statham Way.

A.G. Steel ———————————————————————

RHB & RSM or RFM 1877-93

Born: Liverpool, 24.09.1858 (d. 15.06.1914)

Matches: 47

Batting:

Runs	HS	Av	100s
1,960	105	29.2	1

Bowling:

Wkts	Av	BB
238	13.1	9-63

Catches: 29

Tests: 13

The leisure time of a practising barrister is limited, especially for his chosen sport. This was a great pity in the case of Allan Steel, who was a most extraordinarily gifted cricketer whose skills should have been displayed for the cricket world to see. His main reputation came from his bowling. As well as being a naturally skilful artist, he was a thinking cricketer who played to a plan. There was a clever change of pace or flight to his delivery. He could spin the ball either way as well as deceiving the batsman with a faster straight ball without apparent change of action. With a rhythmic run to the wicket, he bowled round-arm style with immaculate length and accuracy. He believed spin bowling was more difficult to play than fast: the bowler was more in control of pitch, and the batsman more likely to make grave errors. His astonishing record proved it worked for him on the open wickets of his day.

An attacking right-hand middle-order batsman, Allan Steel was most entertaining and attractive to watch. He would claim his place in a side for that quality alone. One of his favourite strokes was a late cut through the

slips and on occasions he could be unpredictably unorthodox, moving down the pitch to hit fast bowlers for four. To disturb the bowler's rhythm was his aim and he was good enough to do so against the best of his day.

In his time, he considered amateur players made the best captains. An educated mind with a logical power of reasoning would read the game more effectively than one which was comparatively untaught. As a successful captain, Steel made decisions with calm judgement and the wise reasoning of a lawyer who could inspire others with confidence. He was a shrewd manager of men, giving quiet words of advice away from inquisitive ears. Team spirit and confidence were the core of his philosophy. Slovenliness in a player's dress was symptomatic of their attitude, so it was banned and a keen energy to succeed replaced negative values. Captaincy was natural to him but limited leisure time restricted his right to the privilege. Lancashire's tragedy was that he turned out so infrequently for them, often having been invited to play in a major game elsewhere, so popular was his presence. He once remarked that nothing could be more dull or dismal than bowling on a sodden wicket to a stonewaller at a ground like Bramhall Lane in a real Sheffield fog. Allan Steel chose to spend his precious spare time wisely.

When he was sixteen years of age, A.G. was picked for the Marlborough School First XI to play Rugby school at Lord's and as the youngest player scored an attractive 41. Soon he was making centuries and destroying sides with his slow bowling. Captaining the side in his final year at Lord's, he scored 128 and took 12 wickets in the match for 59 runs.

In 1877, at eighteen years of age, he made his debut for Lancashire against Sussex scoring 87. The same year he represented the Gentlemen against the Players at The Oval and took 6 for 60, 9 wickets in the match. A few weeks later he commenced his studies at Cambridge University.

Joining his brother Douglas in the Cambridge XI, A.G. made an immediate impact in his first season of first-class cricket with a mighty and memorable series of performances. Yorkshire were routed by his 13 wickets for 85 runs, then he captured 10 of the Surrey wickets and the MCC were destroyed by his 14 wickets for 80 runs in the match. Even the Australians were beaten by an innings and the inter-university match was soon over with A.G. taking another 13 wickets, including 5 for 11 runs in the second innings.

Lancashire were eager to requisition his services and Allan Steel arrived in July 1878 for the Roses game at Old Trafford. Taking 5 for 49 he was responsible for Yorkshire following on and showed no mercy in the second innings with 9 for 63 to beat the White Rose team by an innings. The following match was against Nottinghamshire whom he destroyed with 6 for 19 and 7 for 53 after a superb top score of 78 from his bat.

Earlier in the season Lancashire played the MCC at Lord's, with A.G. capturing 5 for 12 and 7 for 30 for his county; 7 batsmen were clean-bowled. His average of 8.6 per wicket for Lancashire was astonishing. In total he captured 164 wickets for the season in all his games.

The following year he continued his staggering bowling performances for Cambridge but played only four games for Lancashire including the Roses game when he uprooted the opposition with 11 wickets for only 73 runs; he was by far the most destructive bowler when he played. Captaining the Cambridge side in his third year, in seven matches he

dismissed 50 batsmen and scored a century himself against Surrey. Always in the limelight, A.G. at twenty-one years was chosen to play in the first ever Test match to be played in England at The Oval. Against the Australian best he scored 42 in his only innings and took 5 wickets in the match.

In his last year at Cambridge, it was agreed he should represent his university against his county in the inaugural game at the new Aigburth ground, Liverpool, the place of his birth. It was the only game Lancashire lost, because Allan Steel in his usual devastating mood took 6 for 22 and after inviting Lancashire to follow on, continued with 5 for 69. But Steel's allegiance to the Cambridge XI had ended and he joined his native Lancashire for the rest of the season. He took them to the top to claim champion county in 1881, undefeated in the Championship games. A.G. finished top of the batting with an average of just over 50 to complement his excellent bowling.

More brilliant performances followed in the big matches he chose, including his 171 for the Gentlemen of England against his old university. Invited to join Ivo Bligh's England side to Australia, he headed the batting averages for all eleven-a-side matches and was top wicket-taker with 150 wickets at only 6.5 runs per wicket.

Allan Steel played in the first-ever Test match at Old Trafford in 1884 and in the following Test, the first ever at Lord's, he scored 148. He had an average of 55 against the Australians and the best average in the country that season. The same year all four cricketing brothers in the Steel family played together for Lancashire at Aigburth against Surrey.

Under his captaincy two years later, England beat Australia in all 3 Test matches. A.G. was a QC at twenty-seven years, finding less time to play cricket. He served on the Lancashire Committee for many years. A brilliant all-round cricketer, he scored 6,759 runs and took 781 wickets at just 13.5 runs each. Any team would have been successful with this brilliant and talented all-rounder in their side.

Frank Sugg
RHB, 1887-99

Born: Ilkeston, 11.01.1862 (d. 29.05.1933)

Matches: 235

Batting:

Runs	HS	Av	100s
9,620	220	26.5	15

Bowling:

Wkts	Av	BB
10	25.9	2-12

Catches: 131

Tests: 2

Any sportsman with a CV which included playing Test matches for England, captaining Sheffield Wednesday FC, Derby FC and Burnley FC and playing for Everton and Bolton Wanderers as well as winning prizes for long-distance swimming, rifle shooting, bowls, shot put, weight lifting and reaching the final of an amateur billiards championship, must be someone rather special.

Frank Sugg held the record for throwing the cricket ball great distances as well; he was a powerfully built athlete who could crack a ball to the boundary from the start of his innings. A cocktail of orthodox and unusual strokes brought him quick runs and, possessing a good eye and gifted body coordination, he was seldom in trouble with the unorthodox shots. Against Somerset at Taunton, George Baker and he put on 50 in just 3 overs, Sugg hitting 5 fours in 1 over.

In a match at Bristol, Frank Sugg hit 33 fours in a personal total of 220 out of 335 against W.G. Grace's side to win the game by an innings. He opened the innings in this devastating display of hard hitting, made in just over three and a half hours. This included the rare century before lunch on the second day. Against Yorkshire the following year he hit a magnificent century on a difficult wicket facing a strong bowling side for Lancashire to win by an innings. He helped Lancashire win the Championship that season.

A popular player who emptied the bars, he was granted a benefit game in 1897 against Kent. Lord Harris was playing after a long absence from the Kent side. The crowd for the first day was almost 22,000. It rained the second and third so a bumper benefit was lost. Sugg received only £1,000.

The money was placed wisely in a sports outfitters and his business spread from Liverpool to Sheffield and Leeds. He was well known in the football world as well as having played 2 Tests for England against Australia under the captaincy of W.G. Grace. His success in so many other sports guaranteed many admirers who flocked to his shops to meet the famous sportsman. The family business was supported by his cricketing brother Walter, who played for his native Derbyshire.

Born: Bolton, 17.08.1922

Matches: 277

Batting:

Runs	HS	Av
1,786	58	9.7

Bowling:

Wkts	Av	BB
1,168	17.3	9-40

Catches: 118

Tests: 16

Only one spinner has taken 1,100 post-war wickets for Lancashire. Off-break bowler Roy Tattersall, bowling with his best friend Brian Statham, was the man who achieved this statistic. Roy came to Lancashire as a medium-fast seam swing bowler and was very successful in his Bolton League clubs of Tonge and Bradshaw. He lived between the two. Invited to play for Lancashire Seconds in 1947, he was elevated to the First XI the following year and opened the bowling attack with the experienced Dick Pollard. Roy took a Glamorgan wicket with his fourth ball. Watching the young 6ft 3ins athletic bowler was the wise Harry Makepeace, as knowledgeable as any coach in the world. Persuading Roy to bowl off-spin instead of medium pace changed his first-class career. From 32 wickets in the 1949 season, Roy captured 193 first-class victims the following summer with 171 wickets for Lancashire at an astonishing average of 13. This inspirational move resulted in a run of form that broke all post-war records and took Roy to the top of the national averages.

Included in this phenomenal season were 5 Championship matches with 10 wickets or more in the match. Good performances against all counties took Lancashire to the top of the Championship table on 18 July and they were never deposed. Rain interfered with their penultimate game of the season, allowing Surrey to share the Championship title.

Roy represented the Players against the Gentlemen at Lord's and further recognition came when he was called up to tour Australia with the England side. He topped the bowling averages in all first-class matches on the tour with 33 wickets averaging 17.

Roy had altered his style to suit Australian conditions, cutting the ball on hard, dusty wickets rather than spinning it. Re-adjusting his style the next summer for Lancashire was not easy after bowling continuously for over twelve months. He had bowled over 1,400 overs the previous summer and continued without a major break through the winter. Although tiredness crept in, Roy continued his success with 121 first-class wickets, averaging 18. He represented the MCC against the touring South Africans, taking 8 for 51 in their first innings and in the Second Test at Lord's captured 12 wickets for 101 to beat the tourists by 10 wickets. Playing in a total of 16 Tests with 58 wickets, he averaged 26 and would have played many more but for fierce competition from Jim Laker.

Tall and slim with an easy spinning action, Roy had the ability to vary spin, length and speed. He had learnt that variety was necessary in his seam-bowling apprenticeship. His high delivery negated the need to toss the ball high; it came through quickly with bounce, an asset valued by all bowlers. Difficult to drive, just short of a length, the batsman often found

a trio of slip catchers who were as good as any: Grieves, Edrich and Ikin.

In 1952, Roy took 8 for 28 in his first game of the season against Kent in 22 overs, 11 of them being maidens and taking 13 wickets in the match. Once again he topped the Lancashire bowling averages with 130 Championship wickets averaging 17.

The following season he took another exceptional haul of 164 first-class wickets averaging 18. The season included a superb spell against Nottinghamshire with 9 for 40 in the first innings, Bob Berry dismissing the No.9 batsman to spoil all ten. Roy took 14 wickets

in the match against Sussex and 5 for 80 in the game against Australia at Old Trafford. Somerset's Bertie Buse chose Lancashire as opponents for his benefit game at Bath. Tattersall ruined his plans, taking 13 wickets for 69 runs. No Somerset player reached double figures in the first innings with Roy taking 7 for 25. The match was over on the first day before 6 o'clock and the popular Somerset all-rounder retired at the end of that season to continue work outside of county cricket.

More successes came along for Roy Tattersall, who continued to reach the 100-wicket mark in 8 seasons. Usually batting at the end of the order, he made some useful scores including a half century against Leicestershire in a partnership of 105 with Alan Wilson.

For some unknown reason, Washbrook rested him from the side in the late 1950s when he was still bowling well and, after a joint benefit with Malcolm Hilton in 1960, Roy left to be professional at Kidderminster in the Birmingham League. The MCC invited him back four years later for a centenary game against his county. He proved Lancashire had released him too early by taking 6 for 63 in the first innings.

Settling in Kidderminster, he worked at the famous Brintons carpet firm. Later the bowler's scourge of hip trouble meant he had five replacements. Roy has been rightly honoured with a Vice-Presidency at Lancashire and was elected President of the Lancashire Players' Association, reflecting the great respect and fondness felt by his fellow professionals.

Ernest Tyldesley
RHB, 1909-36

Born: Worsley, 05.02.1889 (d. 05.05.1962)

Matches: 573

Batting:

Runs	HS	Av	100s
34,333	256*	45.2	90

Bowling:

Wkts	Av	BB
6	55.3	3-33

Catches: 275

Tests: 14

George Ernest was the younger brother of J.T. by fifteen years. The older Tyldesley had built his reputation at Old Trafford when young Ernest started playing in the same village team at Roe Green. Following his famous brother, Ernest progressed to Worsley before being invited to play for Lancashire Seconds in 1906. The brothers played together for the first time in a match at Liverpool against Warwickshire. Ernest made his first-class debut, followed his brother in at No.5 and the two put on 43 before J.T. retired hurt. His captain, the noble Archie MacLaren, joined him and the new partnership quickly blossomed, adding 125 in just over one and a half hours. Lancashire won by an innings. It gave the lordly MacLaren some perception of the determined qualities of Ernest when unfair expectations must have been a handicap, having a near genius as a brother. Pleased with his impressive debut Ernest listened to the encouraging advice of his older sibling.

The brothers, both right-handed batsmen, were different in style and character. Ernest was less aggressive although he occasionally savaged a fast bowler with superb hooking. Patience, determination and modesty were qualities Ernest possessed and he portrayed them with a well-mannered, gentlemanly nature which attracted many admirers. He would amass thousands of runs without showing spectacular showmanship. Selling light bulbs through the winter months fitted well with his personality. There was no outward ambition to stand out from the crowd but it was important to him that he took part in contributing alongside his colleagues. This quiet, elegant cricketer, with a sensitive nature, believed he should never take advantage of the respected amateur. He knew his place in the social world of the early 1900s and slowly earned the respect of team mates; more importantly he was a reliable, quick player with an efficient range of textbook shots around the wicket. A run accumulator with consistent performances, he soon gathered admirers and after service in the First World War army his statistics became increasingly impressive. In the final count he reached 38,874 first-class runs, more than any other Lancastrian. His county average of over 45 proves his dependability, stamina and value to his team.

The Cricketer magazine of August 1921 describes Ernest's free and beautiful batting style, which didn't contribute to the score with the lightning rapidity of his older brother but had a certain element of calm and refinement, as 'polished'. The perceptive Plum Warner observed his cool, patient, steady mannerisms and his stance at the wicket which evoked a unique sereneness. His movement was not strained. Strong on the off side, he specialised in drives between mid-on and mid-wicket and he entertained with an elegant late cut. He

became a brilliant player of spin and although the best of fast bowlers made him feel uncomfortable occasionally, he patiently waited with sound defence and good technique.

Large crowds supported the Tyldesleys in the regeneration of cricket in 1919. Ernest was physically stronger after four years in the Army. Both scored well over 1,000 runs for the county, Ernest topping the averages. He was thirty years of age and his brother in the twilight of his career at forty-five. Members were robbed of a period when the brothers would have given Lancashire success. The following season Ernest scored his first double century at Edgbaston, the first of 7. Picked for England against Warwick Armstrong's powerful Australians, he made a battling, unbeaten 78 at Old Trafford in the drawn Test. Selected for only 14 Tests, he scored 990 runs with 3 centuries and finished with an excellent average of 55 in all Tests, a statistic to question the strategy of selectors. Many thought he should have been given more international experience. His most successful period was against South Africa when he played in all 5 Tests scoring a century at Johannesburg and another at Durban. He scored the first ever Test century against the West Indies at Lord's in 1928.

His major contribution was to Lancashire cricket over a lengthy period, 573 matches for his county. Managing to break or equal most records, he included 7 hundreds in 7 consecutive matches in 1926, scored 102 centuries in all first-class games and made a third of these after he was forty years of age. He played in all the 5 Championship-winning teams of 1926, 1927, 1928, 1930 and 1934 and topped the batting averages in those years four times out of five. Achieving 1,000 runs in a season 19 times, he topped 2,000 runs in first-class cricket 6 times. His best year was 1928 when he passed 3,000 runs, a Championship year when the team was unbeaten. At the age of forty-five he scored almost 2,500 runs with an average approaching 60.

Many remarkable innings were achieved for his county but one pleased him immensely. A strong Surrey side at The Oval in 1923 had forced Lancashire to follow on and with 4 wickets down still needed 117 runs to avoid an innings defeat. Hobbs and Fender knew of Ernest's fine qualities and he was still at the wicket on the last day. One of the most brilliant innings of the season followed. Never offering a chance, he batted for five hours, hooking and pulling with remarkable effectiveness on a poor wicket and driving through the covers to reach 236. It was too much for the opposition and the game was saved.

Towards the end of his career, Ernest was considered for the role of captain of his county. He had offered to play as an amateur but the Committee in their wisdom chose a Cambridge University man, Lionel Lister, an amateur from a wealthy shipping family. He held no grudges and continued to serve his beloved county by becoming the first professional player on the Lancashire Committee. He retired to the peaceful Rhos-on-Sea where he died at seventy-three years of age.

Throughout his illustrious career his natural modesty would prevent him from mentioning his prolific scores but his powerful presence in the history of Lancashire cricket is a deafening statistic. Ernest was a special cricketer.

Born: Worsley, 22.11.1873 (d. 27.11.1930)

Matches: 507

Batting:

Runs	HS	Av	100s
31,949	295*	41.3	73

Bowling:

Wkts	Av	BB
2	85	1-4

Catches: 311

Tests: 31

A great batsman is to be judged not merely by his scores but by the quality of opposition he faced and the condition of pitches on which he played. J.T. faced bowlers who would be listed with the best of any era, including Lohmann, Richardson, Peel, Noble, Hearne and Rhodes.

Regarded by many as the best of all Lancashire batsmen, John Thomas was a small man, only 5ft 6ins, but powerful, aggressive and quick-witted with a variety of strokes all round the wicket. His favourite stroke was the square cut. After surveying the field he would often lift the ball over the fielders, not afraid to improvise. J.T. was a run collector like Bradman, a stern and resolute player like Barrington, a great improviser like Fairbrother at his best. He was recognised as the best batsman in the country along with Hobbs on sticky wickets.

As a young boy, J.T. played for Roe Green, learning his cricket on the village green. He moved to nearby Worsley when eighteen, then Rusholme and finally to the higher competition in the Bolton League at Little Lever. Invited to play for Lancashire Seconds in 1894, he made his first-class debut the following season at Old Trafford in July against Gloucestershire under the strong leadership of Archie MacLaren. It was as far removed from village cricket as can be imagined. Down the steps from a brand new imposing pavilion opened that season, he followed his team mates led by the lordly MacLaren who had

scored a record 424 the previous match. There was a strict regime and traditions to understand. Eight of the Gloucestershire side were amateurs, gentlemen treated with great respect from the authorities in a superior manner with better changing facilities and separate dining areas. J.T. was a working professional earning his living from the game. The first sight he had of an opposing batsman was the stately walk of Dr W.G. Grace, such an eminent and noble figure assuming the leadership of all English cricket. J.T., small in stature, would have been ignored, but not for long. He watched the powerful man bat until after lunch and later the same day J.T. made his mark batting on a poor pitch. In his second game at Edgbaston, batting at No.5, he scored the only century in the game, an unbeaten 152. The match was won by an innings.

MacLaren was an astute judge of a fine player. John Thomas, the first Tyldesley to play for Lancashire, became a permanent fixture. Sound sensible batting and wise support from captains MacLaren and A.N. Hornby developed confidence in the young Lancastrian. His professional colleagues, Albert Ward, Frank Sugg and Johnny Briggs, all England players, gave him sound advice.

Such a strong batting presence brought Lancashire the Championship two years later.

J.T. scored a century in each innings against Warwickshire at Edgbaston, sharing the distinction with only six previous batsman including Grace, MacLaren and Ranjitsinjhi. He followed with a third consecutive century, making 174 against a strong Sussex side, and went on to score 1,000 runs, repeating this achievement in 19 consecutive seasons with incredible consistency.

Tyldesley was selected to tour South Africa in 1898/99 under the captaincy of Lord Hawke, scoring a century in his second Test at Newlands, Cape Town. By the turn of the century, he was well established in the England side. Extremely quick-footed, seeming to have plenty of time to play his shots, he based his attack on first establishing a sound, well-organised defence and often outshone his partners on poor surfaces. Helped by his brilliant outfield work, he became an automatic Test selection for a decade.

Thought by many to be England's strongest side, MacLaren's 1902 Test team played Australia at Edgbaston. Tyldesley scored 138 and when the Australians were dismissed for 36, still their lowest Test score, 240 behind, they were saved by rain. J.T. was the only professional in a batting line-up including MacLaren, F.S. Jackson, Jessop, C.B. Fry and Ranjitsinjhi. The little Lancastrian was elected Wisden's Cricketer of the Year.

On his third tour to Australia with Plum Warner in 1903/04 he scored a magnificent 62 on a poor, rain-affected pitch. Requiring much skill to remain at the crease, he was most proud of that innings. Selected for 31 Tests between 1898–1909, he played regularly for Players *v.* Gentlemen and scored a century in both innings for the North *v.* the South.

His first-class record reached almost 38,000 runs averaging over 40 with 86 centuries. His popularity among the Lancashire public was proved in his successful benefit match in 1906. Yorkshire was his choice, visiting Old Trafford, and the huge crowds recognised his valued qualities with a bumper record sum at that time of £3,105. He remained on the staff until he was almost fifty years old when he was recalled to captain the side against Yorkshire, standing in for the absent Jack Sharp.

Retiring in 1923 to develop his business, J.T. had invested some finance in a sports outfitters in Deansgate, Manchester. The firm became a household name in sportswear for decades. He was a careful and wise businessman, investing money in buildings. Ten houses built by his brother Frank still exist today in Roe Green. In his spare time he would choose ballroom dancing to keep him fit and retain his balance and nimbleness of foot. J.T. was offered the role of coach on retirement to continue his Lancashire connection, replacing MacLaren. J.T.'s salary was £300, over £200 less than his amateur former captain.

John Tommy was teetotal, a non-smoker and a regular churchgoer. In 1930, just after his fifty-seventh birthday, he was preparing to go to his shop, bent down to put on his boots and collapsed. The great man is buried at St Mark's Church in Worsley.

Dick Tyldesley

RHB & RA (spin), 1919-31

Born: Westhoughton, 11.03.1897
(d. 17.09.1943)

Matches: 374

Batting:

Runs	HS	Av	100s
6,126	105	15.7	1

Bowling:

Wkts	Av	BB
1,449	16.6	8-15

Catches: 322

Tests: 7

A cheerful, red-faced Friar Tuck-like character, Dick Tyldesley was a persistently accurate leg-break bowler. He could vary his length and spin, occasionally turning it both ways and adding a top-spinner which went straight on after pitching. A variety of balls came out of his hand with an exaggerated twist and, uncommonly for a leg-break bowler, moved off the pitch quickly. Seldom did the ball turn much under normal conditions but on a helpful drying pitch he was devastating.

His father, Big Jim, was a massively built, much respected league club captain and professional with Westhoughton. He had four sons who played for Lancashire. Bill, Jim, Harry and the youngest and most successful, Dick. They were no relation to the Tyldesleys of Roe Green a few miles away. Big Jim and his son had broad Lancashire accents as well as broad girths; they liked a pint. Young Richard enjoyed his cricket from youth, coached by his father to drop the ball accurately on a marked spot. He clean-bowled his first 3 victims at Northampton on his Lancashire debut.

In his third year at the county club he achieved 100 first-class wickets, raising the season's total to 184 in 1924 at an awesome average of under 14 runs each. That was his best year. In an astonishing match at Leeds, Yorkshire needed only 57 in their last innings to win, but in just over an hour, Dick Tyldesley took 6 for 18 (10 in the match) and they were bowled out for 33 runs. More prodigious performances were achieved that season. He

brought up his hundredth wicket by taking 5 wickets for no runs against Leicestershire. He took 10 wickets against Warwickshire, 11 against Surrey, 11 at Leyton and 12 against the South African tourists.

Rewarded with a Test call, he played in 4 out of 5 Test matches against the South Africans. Making an unsuccessful England tour of a Australia he had to wait five years to be selected again, making 7 Tests in all.

Dick Tyldesley was fourth highest wicket-taker for his county with 1,509 first-class wickets at an average of 17. As a lower-order right-hand batsman, he could use his weight to crack a ball over the leg-side boundary. Unfairly accused of being agricultural, he scored a magnificent century in two hours and twenty minutes at Old Trafford against Nottinghamshire, top-scoring in the game with an innings of impressive powerful driving and pulling. There were 15 more half centuries in his first-class career. A good fielder at slip or short leg, he took 328 catches.

League cricket offered him a healthy wage for less toil and he asked the Lancashire Committee for a competetive, but massive, £400 a season whether he played or not. They refused and he finished his cricketing days happily playing for Accrington and then Nantwich, where he won the North Staffordshire Championship twice.

Born: Waterloo, 21.11.1865 (d. 06.01.1939)

Matches: 330

Batting:

Runs	HS	Av	100s
15,392	185	30.9	24

Bowling:

Wkts	Av	BB
65	36.6	6-29

Catches: 140

Tests: 7

In London's Whitechapel, the police were searching the streets for Jack the Ripper. Lancashire County Cricket Club had found a character of much different qualities to strengthen the batting. Albert Ward was a gentleman, intelligent, dependable and honest by nature. His determination and passion for cricket was manifest in his youth when he walked five miles to be coached by John Tye, who was playing for Nottinghamshire. Showing promise as a batsman early in his career, he had trials with Yorkshire having enjoyed success with Hunslet Cricket Club. Chosen for only 4 first-class games, he decided to concentrate on his teaching career and was employed in Lancashire. The county club, noticing his stroke play and temperament at club level, invited him to join them.

Hornby and Barlow were the regular openers; Ward, listed at No.4, made his debut at Lord's against the MCC in May. He made an immediate impact with the top score in the match and praise from many senior cricketers. He returned to Lord's to play Middlesex and top-scored again with a magnificent century in three and a half hours. In his first season Ward topped the averages for all Lancashire matches and the county shared the Championship with Nottinghamshire and Surrey.

His 6ft frame allowed him to have a long reach and a strong defence as well as great strength in his driving. Ward drove with power and was a good cutter of the ball. His patient temperament was ideal for an opening batsman, which he became as the ageing Hornby dropped down the order. In 9 seasons he scored 1,000 runs, 1895 bringing his highest aggregate of 1,790 averaging over 42, remarkable figures in his day.

Albert Ward was chosen to play for England against Australia at The Oval in 1893, scoring 55 to help win the match by an innings. He toured with the MCC to Australia under Stoddart and, opening the innings with MacLaren at Sydney, he scored a magnificent century to help win the rubber. In that tour he scored 219 against South Australia at Adelaide and scored the highest aggregate of runs in first-class matches on the tour. Opening in the final innings of his seventh Test, he made 93 and surprisingly was never chosen for his country again.

Although he never took a first-class wicket until he was over thirty years old, he developed a useful leg-break and captured 6 for 29 against Derbyshire at Glossop. He finished his career with almost 18,000 runs including 29 centuries and taking 71 wickets.

He retired to run a successful sports outfitters in Bolton and lived until he was seventy-three years of age.

Cyril Washbrook
RHB, 1933-59

Born: Barrow, 06.12.1914 (d. 27.04.1999)

Matches: 500

Batting:

Runs	HS	Av	100s
27,863	251*	42.1	58

Bowling:

Wkts	Av	BB
4	67	1-4

Catches: 182

Tests: 37

Stockily built with a lordly strut and aristocratic swagger, Cyril Washbrook stepped down from the pavilion to proudly open the batting for the county of his birth. With his cap sitting at a jaunty angle and his chest thrust forward, he gave the impression of immense confidence and purpose. Most people rate him as Lancashire's greatest batsman since the war and one of the quickest cover points of his time. That arrow-like throw made batsmen hesitate when he policed the covers.

First and foremost he was an uninhibited stroke player, a dominating batsman who dictated to the bowlers from the start. Like most of the best, he was primarily a back-foot player and had a few equals in cutting the ball or hooking contemptuously in cavalier style. With this reputation, the fielding side would place a deep square-leg from the first ball to tempt the hook. Statistics reveal the strategy seldom worked. He had in his armoury a rich variety of strokes which, by their very number, included the unorthodox.

Washbrook joined the Lancashire staff in 1933. The great Sydney Barnes accompanied the youngster into the ground, enquiring if he was a batsman or bowler. S.F. Barnes' priority as coach was to develop bowlers. Batsmen in his mind were much easier to find. Most youngsters wanted to be batsmen and over the years he showed little respect for them. But he was the first to congratulate the young Washbrook when he scored an unbeaten 200 in his first full game for the second team.

Cyril Washbrook was born in Barrow, a village near Clitheroe, on 6 December 1914. As a child he watched his village team, which included Eddie Paynter who was playing as an amateur. The youngster watched open-mouthed and spellbound at the quick feet and skilled strokeplay of the small left-handed Lancastrian. He became his hero in childhood and remained so for life.

At eleven years of age, Washbrook was chosen to play in the Barrow Second XI at Darwen, a child among twenty-one men. The opposition smiled, assuming the away team had struggled to find eleven men. Young Washbrook scored his first half century and came home, his pockets laden with coppers – 12s 8d – his first collection. The team captain forecast he would play for England and wrote to Cyril's parents to say so.

Mr Washbrook Snr, a calico printer, moved with his family to Shropshire. The Washbrooks found there were few cricket facilities around their home so cricket stumps were painted on a wall and accurate throwing was practised, as was catching the rebound, which was a Bradmanesque activity. Within a few years at Bridgnorth School the centuries came, over 1,300 runs in a season at sixteen years of age.

Offers came from Lancashire, Warwickshire and Worcestershire, but his heart was with his home county and that early vision of Eddie Paynter. He was soon representing his county in the Second XI at Bradford. In the Yorkshire side was a young Len Hutton. Cyril scored 202 with an encouraging Bill Farrimond as his partner. Unfortunately Hutton was out for a duck.

The following week he was chosen to play in the First XI against Sussex and then Surrey at Old Trafford where their captain Percy Fender was watching the youngster closely. He told the Lancashire captain, Peter Eckersley, during the interval, that if the young man kept hitting against the spin he would soon be out. Washbrook carried on in his inimitable style and scored 152, the top scorer in the game. Ernest Tyldesley was his partner who smiled gently and encouraged the variety of shots from the eighteen-year-old. Washbrook was called in to the committee room to see the chairman and expected to be congratulated. Instead he was warned not to wear a coloured belt again or to flaunt his cap at an angle. Only the former was changed.

During the long winter, jobs were difficult to find due to the worldwide recession. Offers came from football clubs including Manchester United, Manchester City and Liverpool inviting trials but the youngster returned home to Bridgnorth, deciding to concentrate on developing his cricket skills. It was to pay off, for Washbrook was soon opening with his hero Eddie Paynter. In July 1937 the two put on an opening stand of 268 at Hove and the selectors took note. Paynter was injured and Washbrook was his replacement in the Third Test at The Oval against New Zealand. A young Denis Compton also made his debut.

Washbrook considered his finest innings to be that against Gloucestershire the following year. On a sticky wicket with the ball rising shoulder high and the spinners achieving lift and turn, he made 219 not out and an undefeated half century in the second innings. The prolific Tom Goddard with 6 wickets in the first innings could not dislodge the young professional.

The war years robbed many players of their best years. Cyril became a physical training instructor in the RAF and married Marjory. When a full programme of cricket commenced in 1946, Eddie Paynter had retired. Winston Place became his new opening partner. Their unbeaten 350 opening stand against Sussex is a great highlight. With Len Hutton as his England partner, the two were to produce one of the best opening partnerships in English cricket. Altogether they made 8 opening stands of more than 100, 5 against Australia. When touring South Africa in 1948/49, they set up a record Test opening partnership for England of 359 in the exhausting heat of Johannesburg, still a record today.

In 1956 Cyril Washbrook was appointed a Test selector. The touring Australians had won the Second Test at Lords and the English batting needed strengthening. His co-selectors, knowing his extraordinary qualities, recalled him after five years' absence at forty-one years of age to the Test side at Headingley. When he came in to bat England were 17 for 3. Captain Peter May, still at the crease, could imagine no more reassuring sight than that of the determined and courageous Washbrook. They batted all day, Cyril being out LBW to Benaud just 2 runs short of his century. The Yorkshire crowd gave him a tumultuous reception that he never forgot and England won the crucial Test match and the Ashes.

In 1948, the Lancashire Committee granted Washbrook a benefit match against the Australian tourists. The generous Bradman did not enforce the follow-on, scoring a century in his last appearance at Old Trafford. The Lancashire crowds flocked in to see the Australian captain and to pay tribute to their local hero. He was rewarded with a record benefit of £14,200.

Cyril Washbrook became the first professional captain of Lancashire after ninety years of amateur tradition. He served on the Committee, was elected President and awarded the CBE for services to cricket. He has become part of Lancashire's rich heritage. The upper section of the two-tier stand has been dedicated to the man who will always be remembered as a great entertainer. He was a spectator's batsman who brought sunshine to our summers.

Wasim Akram
LHB & LFM, 1988-98

Born: Lahore, 03.06.1966

Matches: 91

Batting:

Runs	HS	Av	100s
3,168	155	24.3	4

Bowling:

Wkts	Av	BB
374	21.6	8-30

Catches: 23

Tests: 103

Wasim signed for Lancashire in 1988 and made his debut at Trent Bridge at twenty-one years after an impressive three years in Test cricket for Pakistan. He announced his arrival in his second Championship game against Somerset with his maiden century. At Southport he took 5 for 15 in his first spell against Surrey, including a hat-trick, then hit 98 from 78 balls before being caught on the boundary trying to hit a six to win the game. His first season's best analysis was achieved at Northampton taking 7 for 53. The following season he topped the bowling averages including 10 wickets in the Roses game at Old Trafford. In addition there were 27 wickets at 14 to help win the one-day league.

His action was all arm and wrist, the fulcrum being the shoulder rather than the wrist. He would perform an economic run-up, a late scamper and then the left arm whipped the ball across the batsman, short of length, climbing shoulder high. The next would be a devastating in-swinging Yorker. There was no advantage from English conditions to assist, it happened all over the world. He was a truly great bowler who could clean up the innings as well as skittling the openers. His side-on bowling action, whippy arm and strong wrist movement generated extra pace. He could move the ball both ways, which made him the most feared of all pace bowlers in the 1990s. He is the first and only player to take well over

400 wickets in Test matches and 500 wickets in one-day internationals.

His body strength made his batting destructive on occasions. It was the pace at which the runs came that won many matches for Lancashire, particularly in one-day games. In the 1990 Benson & Hedges final, he hit the ball from Neal Radford with a straight drive on to the Lord's pavilion roof. For Pakistan he scored an unbeaten 257 against Zimbabwe in 1996, still the record score for a No.8 batsman in Tests.

He led the Pakistan team for many years through difficult times with accusations of ball-tampering and match-fixing. Proving to be one of the best captains, he led the Pakistan team to win the World Cup in 1992, winning the Man of the Match award. He collected 15 gold awards.

His very presence and positive attitude on and off the field made him an inspirational captain of Lancashire in his final season. He led the team to win the NatWest Trophy and they were AXA National League one-day champions as well as runners-up in the County Championship. A popular, generous man, he donated part of his successful benefit to the children's medical unit at Stepping Hill Hospital.

Mike Watkinson

RHB & RM, 1982-1999

Born: Westhoughton, 01.08.1961

Matches: 298

Batting:

Runs	HS	Av	100s
10,683	161	26.8	11

Bowling:

Wkts	Av	BB
720	33.6	8-30

Catches: 151

Tests: 4

The homely community cricket club of Westhoughton, five miles from Bolton, has produced four English Test players, the fourth being Mike 'Winker' Watkinson. Playing in their First XI at fifteen years of age, the early success brought him offers to become professional at other league clubs and he took this responsibility at British Aerospace in the Bolton League. Mike represented the Lancashire Federation and manager Jack Bond was influential in bringing him to the Lancashire County Club. He played his first First XI game as an amateur along with Neil Fairbrother. The two were the last amateur players to represent the county in 1982; they both signed contracts as professionals the following season.

'Winker' was always immaculately turned out on and off the field. The tidy locker was associated with the well-organised owner. Tall and handsome, there was never a more dedicated Lancastrian. He was a natural leader who could not tolerate second-rate attitudes to the game. There was a strong, dry sense of humour accompanied by determination, purpose and pride at representing his county.

Earning his place in the side as an in-swing bowler, accurate and varying from medium, he took two 6-wicket hauls in his first full season. He could crack the ball hard as a lower-order batsman, very quickly moving up the order and making his maiden century at Southport against Surrey when he was twenty-four years old. Still in his twenties, he won the Man of the Match award in the first Refuge Cup final,

followed by another in the Benson & Hedges final at Lord's in 1990 and another winner's medal in the NatWest final.

Winker was developing into a reliable and competent all-rounder. Appointed captain of his county in 1994, he became only the third Lancashire player to score a century and take 10 wickets in a match. He had scored 1,000 runs and taken 50 wickets the previous season and was high on the county's list of all-rounders.

The mid-1990s brought him more success. As captain he lifted the Benson & Hedges cup at Lord's in consecutive years, leading them to the double cup-winning side six years earlier. He made his England debut in 1995, taking 5 wickets in the match at Old Trafford and with the bat an unbeaten 82 at Trent Bridge. The same season he made his top score of 161 against Essex and was chosen to tour South Africa with the England side the following winter. Further success came as he developed an accurate slow off-break.

A genuine all-rounder for Lancashire, he totalled well over 10,000 runs as well as more than 5,000 in one-day cricket. Add over 700 first-class wickets plus 350 one-day victims and 156 catches as an excellent fielder and it all proves that his valuable contribution to Lancashire was immense. He was a respected captain and coach and, to hold on to his valuable influence at Old Trafford, the Committee appointed him overall manager of cricket in 2002.

Born: Cambridge, 04.11.1844 (d. 26.10.1920)

Matches: 283

Batting:

Runs	HS	Av
4,187	74	12.4

Bowling:

Wkts	Av	BB
1,308	13.3	9-118

Catches: 261

'Sandy' Watson's bowling was so accurate that he went through one innings without the keeper handling the ball. In twenty-three seasons with Lancashire he seldom missed a match and never delivered a wide. He bowled a formidable off-break and could keep an accurate line and length even bowling against a strong wind.

In his youth he worked in an ironworks near his birthplace eight miles east of Glasgow. Disliking the work, he took every opportunity to play outdoor games and he was chosen to play against the touring All England side in Glasgow when he was twenty years old. Rusholme, a big Manchester club with a good ground, appointed him cricket professional at twenty-four years. Two years later he joined Lancashire as an all-rounder who could keep wicket on occasions. A.N. Hornby was the captain throughout his Lancashire career and Alec's skill with the ball was quickly realised. Taking the ball late in the match against Yorkshire at Old Trafford, he took 2 quick wickets for 5 runs to win the game. On the return match he opened the bowling, going for only a run an over and taking 6 wickets in the match. The following year he took 9 wickets in the Roses match, 11 against Derbyshire and bowled throughout the innings without a break against Surrey. On twelve occasions he bowled unchanged throughout both innings.

Well established in the side as an opening bowler with Bill McIntyre by 1874, he dropped down the batting order. For one match that year he opened the batting with Barlow and scored 53 at Derby. In the return match he took his best analysis of 9 for 118, the other batsman being run out. Four years later he clean-bowled W.G. Grace at Clifton. His analysis was impressive each year, 98 times he took 5 wickets in an innings.

Topping the Lancashire averages on numerous occasions and achieving 100 wickets in all matches in 3 seasons when games totalled less than 20, he was never picked for England. Always a popular player with colleagues, there was a hint of suspect action, although he was never no-balled nor was there ever a complaint against him. When all bowlers in England were scrutinised at the end of the century, Sandy had retired from playing.

Lancashire granted him a benefit in 1885 when he received over £1,000. Taking 1,383 victims in all Lancashire matches at an average of 13.3, he was the first man to take a first-class hat-trick for Lancashire against a strong Kent side. Sandy Watson retired to coach at various schools including Marlborough. He lived in Manchester for the rest of his life running a successful sports outfitters.

Frank Watson

RHB & RM, 1920-37

Born: Nottingham, 17.09.1898 (d. 01.02.1976)

Matches: 456

Batting:

Runs	HS	Av	100s
22,833	300*	37	49

Bowling:

Wkts	Av	BB
402	31.8	5-31

Catches: 287

A successful county side is balanced with players who have creative flair that excites and stimulates the crowds as well as patient accumulators of runs who build solid foundations. Frank Watson was in the latter group. Seldom was he the subject of after-match conversation in the bars where an innings of a flamboyant nature was reflected, embellished by alcohol, but he was seldom missing from the lips of statisticians, so impressive were his figures.

His fellow professionals appreciated his presence. A reliable partner gives confidence to the whole side and encourages freedom of stroke play from other batsmen. Frank Watson's batting was effective, not graceful or artistic; it was patient and dependable, not flimsy and erratic. There was stubborn substance to the first hours of play. Bowlers knew his wicket was a prize to capture.

There were exceptions to his patient run-building. He could drive the ball powerfully, hook well, and he had a late cut which proved productive throughout his career. I recall Cyril Washbrook reminiscing about a Watson innings in a Roses match at Bradford in the mid-1930s when he hit an explosive century in boundaries. Usually his strokes were severely restricted, effectively reducing errors and increasing safety.

As a consistent run-collector he would have played for England had not Hobbs and Sutcliffe occupied that seat for endless years. He did accompany the MCC on a minor tour to the West Indies in the mid-1920s and scored a century at Kingston. Always on the periphery of major honours, he did represent the Players *v.* Gentlemen at Lord's and was called for an occasional Test trial.

In 1928 when the team was undefeated, he shared over a dozen opening stands of a century or more with Charlie Hallows. A partnership of 371 with Ernest Tyldesley for the second wicket against Surrey at Old Trafford the same year is still a record for any wicket. His individual score was an undefeated 300 which was another record at Old Trafford for almost seventy years. Averaging over 68 that year with over 2,400 runs he continued his amazing 2,000-run accumulation for two further seasons.

As decades pass and Watson's contribution is viewed from a distance, his great achievement will be evaluated in a balanced and reasoned context. The Watson/Hallows opening partnership was in its time as prolific and wealthy as MacLaren and Spooner or as popular as Morecambe and Wise with Watson playing the straight man. A useful medium-pace change bowler who could break occasional partnerships, he captured over 400 wickets for Lancashire, but the impressive statistic of 23,596 hard-earned runs is his legacy.

Alan Wharton

LHB & RMF, 1946-60

Born: Heywood, 30.04.1923 (d. 26.08.1993)

Matches: 392

Batting:

Runs	HS	Av	100s
17,921	199	33.5	25

Bowling:

Wkts	Av	BB
225	31.5	7-33

Catches: 223

Tests: 1

Flourishes, flair and frills played no part in a Wharton innings. He was a natural, honest left-handed batsman, a product of the Lancashire leagues. Attacking the bowling from the beginning, Wharton disregarded the Makepeace holy writ that there should be no fours before lunch, especially in a Roses match. If the first ball was a loosener, it was cracked to the boundary unceremoniously and forgotten. He drove straight and pulled strongly and his energetic batting which was mainly off the front foot earned him almost 18,000 runs for his county.

His bowling was meritorious, on occasions most effective and at worst useful. Taking the new ball with Brian Statham, his right-arm medium pace was deceptively sharp. After a sudden agitated spurt of energy halfway through his run, his faster delivery was sent down with honest determination. Against Sussex at Old Trafford in his late twenties he took 7 wickets for 33 to secure an innings win. His total wickets for Lancashire added up to 225 averaging around 30.

Alan Wharton was a fine, reliable fielder anywhere but it was his batting that caught the eye of the Test selector when he scored 3 centuries on the run and was chosen to play for England against New Zealand at Headingley in 1949.

Injured for the following Test, he was never given a second chance. Lancashire gained from his consistent scoring as he reached 1,000 runs in 9 seasons. He thought his best innings for Lancashire was the superb century he scored against the strong Australian side in 1956 which included Lindwall, Miller and Davidson. Three years later he was run out on 199 dashing for his double century at Hove and that season he scored well over 2,000 runs averaging more than 40.

His name will be forever recorded in the statistical annuals for achieving the only Championship win without losing a wicket when he opened each innings with Jack Dyson against Leicestershire. In his late thirties Wharton was asked to captain the Second XI to bring through youngsters to join an ageing team. He refused the job and moved to Leicestershire for three years to score a further 3,000 runs.

A talented athlete as well as all-round cricketer, Alan Wharton played rugby union at Exeter college, full-back for Salford rugby league side and was captain of Colne Golf Club. A church man, schoolteacher and the longest serving JP in the country, he was regarded as a very popular local sporting hero.

Born: Northwich, 05.11.1916 (d. 03.09.2002)

Matches: 63

Batting:

Runs	HS	Av
296	48	8

Bowling:

Wkts	Av	BB
232	26.2	8-53

Catches: 49

Tests: 3

One wonderful summer placed Len Wilkinson in the record books. He was the best young spinner in England in 1938, taking 51 first-class wickets averaging 23, an astonishing achievement by any leg-break bowler at the tender age of twenty-one years. Len seldom erred from perfect length, turning the ball quickly and bowling a disguised googly so deceptively it captured him many wickets. In his first season with Lancashire he topped the Second XI averages easily and took 12 wickets in the challenge match with Surrey to decide the Champion team.

Born in Northwich, he moved to the Bolton area for his early schooling and joined the Heaton Cricket Club at thirteen years, developing as a quick bowler. A tall youth with large hands, he discovered he could spin the ball accurately and bowl the 'wrong'un' effectively and naturally. His rare skill was reported to the legendary coach at Old Trafford, Harry Makepeace, who offered him terms the same day as Winston Place in 1936. Len left his job on the spinning mule at the local mill and made his first-class debut against New Zealand at Old Trafford. In his first over he bowled 'Curly' Page, the Test captain and double international. Finishing the season with 11 wickets in the match against Nottinghamshire, he established his place for the start of his remarkable performance in 1938.

That magical season he competed in every game. He passed his target of 100 wickets in early August and finished with a further 50.

That consistently accurate bowling earned him a place in an England XI at Folkestone and a tour with the MCC to South Africa the following winter accompanying England spinners Doug Wright, Verity and Tom Goddard. Len played in 3 Test matches taking 7 wickets and topped the averages in all tour matches with 44 wickets.

On his return to the county he injured a hand, which restricted him to 63 wickets in 1939. He felt the pressure to perform as an England bowler and tried too hard, he said. There were memorable matches, including 8 for 53 against Hampshire and 5 for 73 against Middlesex. He was proud of dismissing his hero Wally Hammond twice before the Army called for his services as a sergeant physical training instructor during the war. He played only a handful of matches for the Army including a game for the Empire XI when he took 6 for 33.

A cartilage operation in 1946 restricted his playing and he left the county scene to become a league professional with Furness Cricket Club in the north of the county. He ran a newsagent's business before working in the drawing office at Vickers shipyard, Barrow-in-Furness. Retiring at sixty-five years, he enjoyed caravanning in the Lake District and gardening, in spite of hip replacements. He died at home in Barrow aged eighty-five years, leaving a widow and two sons. He is fondly remembered in Lancashire for his special guile, puzzling many great batsmen in his short first-class career.

Alan Wilson
RHB & WK, 1948-62

Born: Newton-le-Willows, 24.04.1920

Matches: 171

Batting:

Runs	HS	Av
760	37*	5.9

Catches: 287

Stumpings: 59

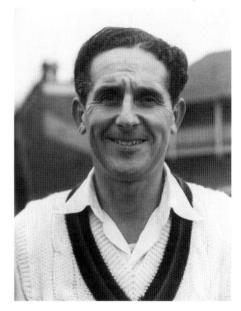

Newton-le-Willows, then in Lancashire, was where Alan first saw light of day, and there he has remained all his life though the bureaucrats have decided it is now in Merseyside. He was wicketkeeper at fifteen years of age for the nearby Earlstown league club when war intervened. After serving in uniform as a Desert Rat in Tobruk, he returned to his old job as a biscuit designer. It was a most unusual profession and one which won him an invitation to appear on the famous TV programme *What's My Line?* Moving league clubs to his own home team, Newton-le-Willows, news reached the ears of Lancashire coach Harry Makepeace who invited him for trials.

Making his debut against Glamorgan at Old Trafford, Alan strutted out to bat as a nightwatchman. Always immaculately dressed, he adjusted his gloves, looked around the field and was immediately bowled. The watching Bill Roberts commented to others in the Lancashire dressing room that he looked like the great Ranjitsinhji going out to bat and the name stuck. In his first season, Ranji played against the 1948 Australians in Cyril Washbrook's record benefit match. The first innings read 'Don Bradman Caught Wilson Bowled Roberts 28'. What a victim to collect, and it was an impressive performance with 4 catches against the Invincibles in a debut season.

Ranji was an efficient keeper, standing back and close to the wicket. He was not demonstrative or extrovert but an effective, keen, dedicated player who worked hard to improve his keeping. Determined to succeed, he rigged up a dummy batsman in the spare room at his home and spent hours taking returns off the wall to the annoyance of his wife. He faced competition for his First XI place throughout his career with Alf Barlow and Eric Edrich in the 1940s and Jack Jordan, Frank Parr and Geoff Clayton in the 1950s. Ranji claimed 346 victims for Lancashire. He equalled the county's wicketkeeping record at that time when he claimed 8 catches against Hampshire at Portsmouth.

This hardworking, popular team man was one of the first Lancashire cricketers to take an MCC coaching course and it led to him being accepted as Stan Worthington's deputy at Old Trafford on the coaching staff. He made his last appearance for his county in June 1962 for his benefit game, receiving a healthy £4,000 reward from the supporters. Ranji kept fit on retirement, playing league cricket for Stockport and badminton during the winter. Keeping a slim figure into his eighties, he was a keen gardener and took up ballroom and sequence dancing as well as keeping a keen eye on Lancashire cricket.

Barry Wood
RHB & RM, 1966-79

Born: Ossett, 26.12.1942

Matches: 260

Batting:

Runs	HS	Av	100s
12,969	198	35.2	23

Bowling:

Wkts	Av	BB
251	27.5	7-52

Catches: 200

Tests: 12

Born the eighth of eleven children to a Yorkshire miner, Barry played early league cricket in the Dewsbury area. He played 5 games over four years for Yorkshire, averaging around 12 runs. His lack of first-team experience forced Barry to try over the Pennines and soon he was in the Lancashire side against Essex in 1966. A year later he scored his first 1,000 runs and became an essential member of the team of fit, aggressive cricketers who dominated one-day cricket in England.

Woody, a blond-haired, cocky, determined batsman with a compact technique, soon moved up the batting order to open the innings. Possessing an endearing confidence, this orthodox right-handed batsman was gifted with the will to win. His competitive spirit and drive to succeed made him an ideal team member. Added to this was his brilliant, athletic fielding, particularly at gully, and an ability to bowl accurate medium-paced delivery which was economical and successful in breaking partnerships. He could cut the ball to make it wobble both ways and in cloudy conditions his movement through the air kept the best of aggressive batsmen quiet, keeping runs to a minimum in the limited-overs game. In 219 one-day games he earned a record 16 Man of the Match awards.

In county cricket, Woody was at his best facing fast bowlers and would regularly pull a short delivery for four. His shot selection was studious, constantly theorising and analysing after an innings. There was a sense of the theatrical when he hit Don Wilson for six to bring up both his centuries in the Roses matches of 1970. He set up a record 5th wicket partnership of 249 with Andrew Kennedy at Edgbaston and shared in over 50 partnerships of over 100, mostly with opening partner David Lloyd. His top score was 198 against Glamorgan at Liverpool in a 290 partnership with Harry Pilling. His enthusiasm was infectious in all disciplines. He believed every ball he delivered was unplayable. He captured 251 first-class wickets with 7 for 52 against Middlesex at his best. There were 219 limited-overs victims too.

His successful performances gave him a deserved England Cup against Australia, scoring 90 in the first of 12 Tests. On a trip to India the following winter he was unwell and failed to dominate the spin attack. In addition he played 13 limited-overs games for England.

There were controversial moments in his career. Believing in his outstanding ability, he thought he was undervalued and went on strike for an increased salary. The members appreciated his valued contribution with a massive benefit in his day. Woody continued to hold strong views and left the county to captain Derbyshire for a short spell, winning a final at Lord's. After scoring 17,433 first-class runs, he played for Cheshire and a variety of league clubs, still with boyish enthusiasm.